On the Doctrine of Election

COLUMBIA SERIES IN REFORMED THEOLOGY

The Columbia Series in Reformed Theology represents a joint commitment of Columbia Theological Seminary and Westminster John Knox Press to provide theological resources for the church today.

The Reformed tradition has always sought to discern what the living God revealed in Scripture is saying and doing in every new time and situation. Volumes in this series examine significant individuals, events, and issues in the development of this tradition and explore their implications for contemporary Christian faith and life.

This series is addressed to scholars, pastors, and laypersons. The Editorial Board hopes that these volumes will contribute to the continuing reformation of the church.

EDITORIAL BOARD

Columbia Theological Seminary wishes to express its appreciation to the following churches for supporting this joint publishing venture:

COLUMBIA SERIES IN REFORMED THEOLOGY

On the Doctrine of Election

With Special Reference to the *Aphorisms* of Dr. Bretschneider

FRIEDRICH SCHLEIERMACHER

Translated with an Introduction and Notes by

Iain G. Nicol
and
Allen G. Jorgenson

Foreword by Terrence N. Tice

 WESTMINSTER
JOHN KNOX PRESS
LOUISVILLE · KENTUCKY

© 2012 Westminster John Knox Press

First edition
Published by Westminster John Knox Press
Louisville, Kentucky

12 13 14 15 16 17 18 19 20 21—10 9 8 7 6 5 4 3 2 1

Book and cover design by Drew Stevens

Library of Congress Cataloging-in-Publication Data

Schleiermacher, Friedrich, 1768–1834.
 [Über die Lehre von der Erwählung. English]
 On the doctrine of election : with special reference to the Aphorisms of Dr. Bretschneider / Friedrich Schleiermacher ; translated, with introduction and notes, by Iain G. Nicol and Allen G. Jorgenson ; foreword by Terrence N. Tice.—1st ed.
  p. cm. — (Columbia series in Reformed theology)
 Includes bibliographical references (p.   ) and index.
 ISBN 978-0-664-23688-5 (alk. paper)
 1. Election (Theology) 2. Reformed Church—Doctrines. 3. Bretschneider, Karl Gottlieb, 1776-1848. I. Title.
 BT810.3.S3513   2012
 234—dc23

2011039956

PRINTED IN THE UNITED STATES OF AMERICA

∞ The paper used in this publication meets the minimum requirements
of the American National Standard for Information Sciences—Permanence
of Paper for Printed Library Materials, ANSI Z39.48-1992.

Westminster John Knox Press advocates the responsible use of our natural resources.
The text paper of this book is made from 30% post-consumer waste.

Most Westminster John Knox Press books are available at special quantity discounts
when purchased in bulk by corporations, organizations, and special-interest groups.
For more information, please e-mail SpecialSales@wjkbooks.com.

To Terrence N. Tice

Indefatigable Schleiermacher scholar,
for his constant support and encouragement

CONTENTS

FOREWORD

On the Doctrine of Election was written in preparation for Schleiermacher's issuing the first edition of his theological *magnum opus, Christian Faith* (1821/22). Readers will find the doctrines that he had come to by then wholly consistent with doctrines systematically presented in its second edition (1830/31). There the doctrines of election and the Holy Spirit are introduced in tandem (§§115–25), then expanded throughout the remainder of the work (§§126–72). I have gladly labored, stage by stage, with Iain Nicol and Allen Jorgenson in their production of this first English edition of an essay that clearly deserves more fame than it has received over the years since Schleiermacher prepared it. It is now a sheer delight to commend their highly accurate, useful, and accessible introduction, translation, and meticulous notes as the essay comes into the light anew.

Schleiermacher's chief aim here is to support the movement toward church union between churches of Lutheran and Reformed heritage (the latter being chiefly Calvinist in doctrine, Presbyterian in polity). Hence, it is both appropriate and impressive that one of the professors who now open this work to a wider readership is a seasoned Reformed theologian (Nicol) and the other a Lutheran theologian (Jorgenson) who is early in what one hopes will be an equally long career, the two having worked closely together throughout, line by line.

I

Readers are invited to work through Schleiermacher's argument in the early parts of this essay, which is set forth with extraordinary precision and clarity, even more so given the much shorter sentences and paragraphing provided by its translators, as well as the headings they added to ease following the course of the argument. Contemporary readers may find the major historical controversy that Schleiermacher has sought to unravel a bit tedious; yet, resolution of the issues involved actually affects every other area of doctrine. As in *Christian Faith*, Schleiermacher takes pains here, as becomes particularly evident in his endnotes, amicably to entertain a great many confessional, traditional, and more recent positions. He does this in order to extract from those tangled webs an authentically grounded reflection on experiences of faith within the church. This reflection, for him, must be one that is in accord with the core, canonical proclamation regarding the redemption that God has accomplished in Jesus the Redeemer. The elements of this proclamation are to be found in the New Testament but have been more or less fruitfully formulated over the ages since then. These diverse formulations have to be sorted out properly if they are to gain genuine currency in the church of any later era.

What is required, then, to follow Schleiermacher's argument? Basically, four things: patience, an elementary sense for logical implication, openness to influence, and, finally, the unwillingness to take unnecessary refuge in paradox, especially when taking refuge in paradox is not clearly warranted in terms of available argument. Warrantable paradoxes do seem to exist, if only quite rarely. For example, the seemingly irresolvable contradiction that lies in the distinction between human free will and natural determinacy, wherewith even a claim of their "compatibility" does not seem to be provable. This issue is a strictly philosophical matter, whereas the controversies over divine election are not. Still, even holding the philosophical paradox concerning beliefs in free will and determinism can be useful for a person engaged in therapy, for a pastor offering care, or even for a person who simply wants to be discerning of another's situation or of one's own. For example, where one is facing a person caught in the grip of some harmful pattern of detrimental behavior, it can be useful to recall that all human behavior is multiply determined. This realization can yield empathy, a nonjudgmental attitude, and a desire to understand. On the other hand, where a person seems to be on the cusp of being able to take responsibility for changing a pattern of behavior, it can be useful to recall that human beings are supposed to possess a degree of free will. This realization, in turn, can yield gentle suggestions, challenges, and attitudes of encouragement and support.

In this essay readers are encouraged to take note of where Schleiermacher deems affirmations of human fault and divine grace among Calvinists and Lutherans to be reconcilable, once he has come to dismiss glaring errors on both sides. These are strictly historical-theological arguments, though they do appropriately draw on logic to sort out those seemingly misbegotten errors. I am confident that the implications for care of souls (*Seelsorge*), which he takes to lie at the foundation of all practically applied theology, will be found to parallel the loving consequences of what can result from the philosophical investigations I just pointed to, only with a potentially greater richness of insight.

II

If a reader wants to know what Schleiermacher advises, paying attention
once he winnows the chaff from the morass of positions, one could skip
to the latter sections: (1) The first of these latter sections, "Election, the
Absolutum Decretum, and Creation," lays out the attainment of a freer per-
sonhood through renewal and self-development, quickened by the divine
Spirit through communal life with others. (2) "Creation and Redemption
Presume One [indivisible] Divine Decree" discusses how faith and blessedness are brought about by grace and how works righteousness is to
be regarded. (3) "Election, the Authorship of Evil, and the Captivity of
Reason" deals with "the presupposition of human incapacity apart from
Christ and his Spirit." Significantly, it further deals with the question of
whether as the final cause of human freedom, as of everything real, God
is also the final cause of human evil or only the author of good, because
such evil does not exist except in terms of the law. Thus, he asks whether
reason should not be content with examining effective causes in nature
and history, not final causes or what creates the oneness of the world as
a whole in which "each particular is both active and at the same time in
process of becoming." The section also deals with questions regarding
"why one person is received into the reign of God and not another," and
where, in the creation of "spiritual life," final and effective causes might
converge.

Then, (4) the thesis that "God in Election Intends the Whole" is taken
to mean the following: Through "proclamation of the Word," amidst the
common spiritual life of the church, the Spirit quickens individuals into
life in that "reign of God"—into that "new creation of the future predestined by God"—within which may be glimpsed "that final instant beyond
the unknown and unpredictable apportionments of progress, when all the
dead will be made alive and every resistance will be taken up into the oneness of the whole." Thus, in this section God's will is equated with God's
love. All human beings are also seen to have equal claims on grace and
an eventual state of blessedness, whereas "the universal fatherly love,"
mercy, and justice of God leaves no room for "damnation to all eternity."
Schleiermacher admits here, moreover, that neither the Calvinist nor the
Lutheran understandings of damnation drives one any more strongly to
this view than the other does. The "difficulties of reconciling eternal damnation with divine love" are seen to be just as great on either side.

(5) "Election and Church Union" closes the essay. Lutherans and
Reformed, he argues—and not only they, of course—can form *one* church
despite differences regarding election and the Lord's Supper. With regard
to election, however, the Formula of Concord is found to bear more intrac-
table conflict within it than does Calvin's *Institutes.*

Schleiermacher's sixty-three endnotes are aptly filled out and translations for his quotations are furnished by the editors. Reading them and the
further brief footnotes also supplied by them will amply repay readers'
attention, for they offer both context and substance to the main account.
Readers will doubtless thank them for their care and perseverance. With
them, I say also: Thanks and glory be to God and to our Redeemer, who
both lives among us and goes before us!

                                                            Terrence N. Tice

ON THE DOCTRINE OF ELECTION:
AN INTRODUCTION

A frequent prejudice infecting facile assessments of the work of Schleiermacher is the assumption that his theology was so thoroughly invested in an uncritical employment of Enlightenment themes and philosophy as to have neither historical nor dogmatic utility for those wishing to engage the mainstream Christian tradition. *On the Doctrine of Election* thoroughly belies this fallacy. In this erudite work, Schleiermacher demonstrates a mastery of the historical, systematic, pastoral, and ecumenical implications this doctrine has for the fledgling union church. Like the best of theologians Schleiermacher faithfully transmits the doctrine in a key appropriate to his time by critically deploying the best of classic texts and epochal movements of the tradition as he explicates the doctrine of election. This introduction first underscores the key themes in the texts referenced by Schleiermacher in *On the Doctrine of Election* to consider how they affect the contour of his argument in preparation for an overview of the text proper. In conclusion we ponder how this monograph arouses the interest of those who engage the doctrine of election in a time such as ours in an effort to revisit the significance of this oft-muted theological locus.[1]

SCHLEIERMACHER AND AUGUSTINE

As a student of the Reformation, it is not surprising to discover Schleiermacher's ready engagement of Augustine in his treatment of the doctrine of election. Augustine was an important source for both Luther and Calvin, both of whom served among the primary resources for Schleiermacher's theology. In addressing the question of election, Schleiermacher makes special reference to Augustine's *On Rebuke and Grace*,[2] which demands some exegesis in order to ascertain its significance for *On the Doctrine of Election*.

On Rebuke and Grace resulted from a practical concern that arose in response to Augustine's devastating critique of Pelagius. The three geographical centers around which this dispute arose were Hippo, Hadrumetum, and Uzalis. In the monastery in Uzalis, around the year 425, a

1

letter from Augustine was found outlining the Catholic doctrine of election in response to the Pelagian controversy. A monk from Hadrumetum who was in Uzalis happened upon this letter and, in his enthusiasm over its contents, brought a copy of it to Hadrumetum. Some of the monks at Hadrumetum were not enthralled by the doctrine of grace expounded in this letter, worrying that it was detrimental to free choice and dismissive of merits or lack thereof by which God would render judgment in the last day. The dispute came to the attention of the abbot at Hadrumetum, who sent monks to Hippo to speak with Augustine regarding the controversy. After instructing these same monks in the themes which gave rise to the letter, Augustine sent them back to Hadrumetum with a copy of the treatise *On Grace and Free Choice*. This work failed to smooth over the problems at Hadrumetum. One of the monks contested the worth of Augustine's exposition of grace, fearing that it made superfluous the Christian practice of rebuking sinners. The monk argued that if God alone is responsible for a will turned to God in such a way that human freedom is eliminated, then there is no point in rebuking the sinner. All that one can do is pray for the person. This reception of Augustine's exposition of grace elicited *On Rebuke and Grace*, the only work by Augustine referenced by Schleiermacher in *On the Doctrine of Election*.

At the heart of Augustine's argument is the theme that predestination precludes neither the possibility nor the necessity of rebuke. Augustine makes a case for this by leading his reader through a series of arguments. First he discloses the errors in the ways of those uninterested in being rebuked. He then establishes the integrity of rebuking sinners by demonstrating that it neither undoes election's corollary of providence nor is undermined by the mysterious character of predestination. Augustine reverts to the example of Adam to clarify the character of the predestining grace operative in the redeemed before explicating the nature of the predestining Christ who chooses the elect (John 15:16). This latter theme leads into the heart of Augustine's treatment of predestination: its very inexplicability bespeaks the humility it engenders as a riposte to the pride that marks the unregenerate. In conclusion, Augustine returns to the theme of rebuke in giving practical advice for this necessary moment in the Christian life. A few comments are in order to demonstrate the significance of this work for Schleiermacher's treatment of election.

From the outset it should be emphasized that Augustine's treatment of rebuke and its relationship to the doctrine of election answers charges of absolute passivism. Rebuke is encouraged because God uses external words to effect internal changes. God is the one who wills change through rebuke, although God is able to do this without rebuke.[3] In sum, grace does not preclude prayer or the rebuke that reproaches those breaking commandments. The divine initiative, in the thought of Augustine, does not preclude human agency even though it is an agency that is used by God. This theme is recalled in Schleiermacher's appeal to a receptive passivity. The theme of predestination, for both Schleiermacher and Augustine, does not preclude the possibility of an ethic, although that which is experienced by us as ultimate is judged to be penultimate by a doctrine of grace.

In addition to underscoring the significance of the manner in which election affirms the graced nature of God's interaction with us, Augustine highlights the importance of the divine use of created realities. He frames the doctrine of election and perseverance by temporal categories. So, for instance, in arguing for the significance of perseverance Augustine notes that God's decision not to allow the death of the backslidden before they fall so that they remain in faith as well as the divine decision to extend the lives of those who have not yet come into grace both point to nonspiritual factors as spiritually significant.[4] Schleiermacher picks up this theme from Augustine in his treatment of the divine decree, one that he exploits to the best of his abilities. The gratuity of election is of a piece with the inexplicability of creation's varied beneficence. That God should make one well and another ill, one short and another tall is no stranger than the mysteriousness of God's electing this one rather than that one. Observations such as these point to the utter gratuity of God's choosing, which produces a doxological "I do not know" in the faithful.[5] Nescience in this regard is deemed a virtue which heightens believers' wonder that freedom is obtained by grace in contrast to the Pelagian counterpoint.[6]

Augustine's whole treatment of perseverance is foundational to this work. He notes, for instance, that God grants rebirth to those to whom he denies perseverance, with the end being their damnation.[7] This mystery merely underlines the fact that perseverance is of a piece with election and that both point to the mysterious nature of grace, which advances by God's good pleasure in bringing good from evil instead of not allowing evil to exist.[8] Moreover, Augustine insists that those who are recipients of God's foreknowledge, predestination, election, and sanctification will most certainly attain beatitude. He insists that even among the fallen, rebuke is warranted as the means by which this salutary pattern is enacted.[9] Augustine recognizes that this theme raises concerns for Christians who consider the example of Adam, who failed to have perseverance despite his beginning in a state better than ours. Augustine affirms that Adam was a special case. He had a free choice that ought to have been exercised in favor of God's intentions. Adam, in short, had the grace of the ability to choose but not yet the grace of willing, this latter being given to the redeemed in Christ.[10] Christians, however, are not to look to Adam, but to Christ, who instantiates the second grace of willing well, the very grace active in the lives of believers. The first Adam was able not to sin, which constituted the first freedom. The second freedom, however, is not to be able to sin.[11] The second Adam has this more powerful grace and with it frees the saints so that "they have free choice by which they serve God, not by which they are held captive by the devil."[12]

In sum, Augustine's treatment of perseverance and predestination decisively eliminates the possibility of pride. There is no place for merit, no room for reward; the saved boast in God alone and the doctrine of election alone protects the blessed in that state by denying occasion for boasting. Further, in this life no one is able to boast of being in the number of the saved. This latter theme makes possible the rebuke by which God effects salvation and inspires the prayer that fires the passion of those whose duty it is to rebuke sinners.

SCHLEIERMACHER, LUTHER, AND LUTHERANISM

Assessing Schleiermacher's reception of the Lutheran treatment of the doctrine of election requires some preparatory work in order to understand the varying positions of Schleiermacher's Lutheran interlocutors. Schleiermacher rightly differentiates Luther from Lutherans on the topic of election, predestination, and their relationship to the evangelical imperative. He was especially aware of different points of emphasis on the question of divine determination as expressed in the thought of later Lutherans as over against Luther's *De Servo Arbitrio*.[13] This text, then, serves well as a starting point for some clarification of Luther's and the Lutheran position on election.

In *De Servo Arbitrio*, Luther speaks of the divine necessity establishing everything as he argues against what he perceives to be the Pelagian tendencies of Erasmus's work. One cannot gainsay, therefore, the importance of the doctrine of election for the thought of Luther. Yet this assessment can be understood only in light of Luther's certainty that various loci can perform the same dogmatic function.[14] This is the reason for Luther's assessment of election as a "sweet" subject.[15] Election names in a different fashion that which is properly identified by justification. It points to the unmerited redemption of the sinner, whose response itself is a gift of grace. Yet what exactly are the contours of this doctrine for Luther, and for those who followed him? It is beyond the scope of this introduction to treat this question exhaustively, yet a handful of comments are in order. Luther's notion of the bound will is of a piece with his assertion that all that happens occurs by divine necessity.[16] This statement had a particular and important function in his argument with Erasmus, but its status in his broader approach to the question of election is somewhat ambiguous. On the one hand, we have his stern warnings in his *Lectures on Genesis* about the dangers of the notion of divine necessity if it is misunderstood and misused.[17] Yet, on the other hand, in his *Lectures on Romans*, in responding to the question whether contingency of an event can impede the work of predestination, Luther asserts that "with God there simply is not contingency, but it is only in our eyes."[18] It is important to note, then, that Luther's own use of the notion of divine absolute necessity is guarded. Robert Kolb suggests the significance of this for Luther's thought as he asks:

> Why was it so little used by his students even though he and many of his students praised it highly? Why did the reformer himself feel compelled to warn against its possible misuse? What elements of the message shaped the thinking of the next generation, and which of its insights slipped from the agenda of the Lutheran theology?[19]

This latter question is especially interesting in light of the history of the development of Lutheran theology following the death of Luther. Luther's partner in reformation, Philipp Melanchthon, did not embrace Luther's notion of divine necessity and underlined the theme of human responsibility on the part of the one already in Christ.[20] These differing points of emphasis did not seem to be a reason for contention between the two thinkers, both of whom saw in the other a theme worthy of attention.[21] Consequently each thinker provided emphases that later became definitive for the Reformation project. Luther's work emphasized God's total responsibility for our salvation, a point with which Melanchthon heartily agreed, while Melanchthon, who struggled to make the Reformation message palatable to Catholic interlocutors, often stressed the fact that this gospel message did not rid Christians of their responsibility for living as Christians. This latter point (shared by Luther especially after the Reformation began to create disarray in Germany) included Melanchthon's strong affirmation that the will moved by God in conversion also undergoes a moving of itself, else it is rather like a stick being pushed fatalistically about, a view decried by Luther and Melanchthon alike. Yet this concern became more pronounced for Melanchthon in his later life after the death of Luther, at which time differing emphases in the thought of each became the basis for two opposing parties in the nascent Lutheran movement.

The theological tensions between these two thinkers, when writ large, threatened to become a chasm in Lutheranism. In part the escalation of differences was due to political realities of the time. In April 1547 the Roman Catholic emperor Charles V defeated the Lutheran Smalcald League and imposed on the Lutheran lands the so-called Augsburg Interim, a temporary ecclesial arrangement undoing the Reformation developments, with the exception of marriage of clergy and the distribution of both kinds in Holy Communion. In response to a request from Moritz, the elector of

Saxony, Melanchthon countered with a document outlining a Lutheran compromise that was deemed to be unfaithful to Luther by some, who felt that he had been betrayed by Melanchthon's willingness to entertain certain Roman rituals that had been abandoned by the Lutherans. At the end of the day, the political winds shifted yet again and Charles was pushed out of Germany, forcing him to negotiate with the German princes. The Peace of Augsburg (1555) was the result, with the affirmation that the confessional adherence of a territory was deemed to be the prerogative of the prince of that region. By then, however, the damage had been done and two schools of thought were well written into the architecture of Lutheran thought. These two schools agreed on many themes, including the most important of all: the centrality of justification by grace through faith. Yet, on important issues, such as the role of the will in salvation and the meaning of real presence in the Eucharist, differences did exist, including some that bore upon the question of election.

Those Lutherans called Philippists (after their fondness for Melanchthon), thinking themselves to be faithful to both Luther and Melanchthon, emphasized the integrity of the human even in the state of falleness as well as the importance of the affirmation of the universal character of the salutary will of God. Opponents to the Philippists, the Gnesio-Lutherans (the self-proclaimed genuine Lutherans), held that Melancthon had strayed too far from Luther. Certain of them even denied the existence of the *imago Dei* in fallen humans.[22] Although this was not universally affirmed, the Gnesio-Lutherans generally held a much more pessimistic view of the human. In reference to the notion of the predestining call, they focused on the particularity of the recipient, in opposition to both Luther and Melanchthon, who had seen predestination as directed to communities as opposed to individuals.[23]

Despite these, and other differences, both the Philippists and the Gnesio-Lutherans affirmed the distinction made by Prosper of Aquitaine, the fifth-century theologian, who distinguished God's foreknowledge and predestination in an effort to affirm Augustine's strong doctrine of grace as well as God's desire for the salvation of all.[24] This allowed early detractors of Luther's treatment of divine necessity to preserve "God's foreknowledge without making him responsible for evil, yet it affirmed that God has chosen those who believed apart from any merit."[25] This development in Lutheran thought opposed Luther, who understood that in God foreknowledge functioned as a creative force rather than as a faculty, which would imply a passive observer.[26] While Luther did not assign God as the author of evil, this treatment of foreknowledge implied it, a point roundly rejected by Melanchthon.[27] These differing points of emphasis in Luther and Melanchthon became more pronounced in the

Philippists and Gnesio-Lutherans. A resolution was needed to fend off the impending implosion of Lutheranism.

Martin Chemnitz was instrumental in resolving the many inter-Lutheran debates.[28] Chemnitz's significance for the second generation of Lutherans has been noted in the well-rehearsed aphorism: "If Martin [Chemnitz] would not have come, Martin [Luther] would not have stood" *(Si Martinus non fuisset, Martinus vix stetisset).*[29] His influence is prominent in the Formula of Concord, a document of the early Lutheran church that sought to resolve points of disagreement between the Philippists and Gnesio-Lutherans. As to the issue of election, the compilation of documents in the *Book of Concord* takes a decisive turn away from Luther's notion of divine necessity by clarifying the distinction between foreknowledge and predestination (Epitome XI.1). God's foreknowledge controls evil while God's predestination is the cause of salvation (Epitome XI.3, 4). Election points to the God who both foresees and causes salvation but not damnation, which is foreknown but not caused by God. The *Book of Concord* thereby intends to emphasize that the doctrine functions to comfort terrified consciences.[30] Moreover, the Lutheran confessors also tied the doctrine of election to the means of grace, since God does not work without means (Solid Declaration XI.76). In contrast to certain readings of some of the documents of Luther, predestination is clearly restricted to those elect to salvation and, in contrast to certain distortions of Melanchthon's thought, it is affirmed that the sinner cannot co-cause election (Solid Declaration XI.88). The interpretive key for understanding predestination—well-rehearsed in the *Book of Concord*, which served as a formative document for Lutheran pastors and theologians—was the assertion that election was a doctrine that belonged under the aegis of the gospel, a point that could not be admitted, in the estimation of the confessors, if there were such a thing as a double election.

In sum, Luther himself advanced a notion of predestination that more nearly approximates that of Calvin in certain of the latter's writings, while roundly rejecting a Calvinian notion of the Eucharist, while Melanchthon does the opposite. Under the tutelage of Cheminitz and others, a middle ground is sought, which hosts the tension of God's universal will to save with the recognition that salvation is wholly the prerogative of God. Consequently, although the notion of a double predestination is rejected in Lutheranism, Schleiermacher rightly notes that its corollaries are contested from the very beginning of the Lutheran conversation. Schleiermacher uses this controversy to advance his goal of demonstrating that Luther laid the groundwork for important developments by Calvin. Moreover, this observation is particularly informative in light of the fact that inter-Lutheran debates always took place against the horizon of other controversies, an especial concern with regard to the doctrine of election, around which Lutherans debated intensely with Calvin and his followers, to whom we will now turn.

SCHLEIERMACHER AND CALVIN

Schleiermacher's debt to Calvin is self-admitted and recurring throughout this monograph. In considering the significance of this debt, however, it is important to dispel certain prejudices regarding the nature of the doctrine of election in the thought of Calvin and its significance for his thought as a whole.

Brian Gerrish has noted that in its entirety the *Institutes* sets out the doctrine of the human and God.[31] Insofar as anthropology and theology meet in Christology the christocentric nature of Calvin's thought cannot be gainsaid.[32] It is important to underscore this point in order to unsettle any assessment of Calvin that would displace Christology as the center of his theological project with the doctrine of election. Just as justification does not displace Christology in Luther's theology, but serves as the foundational interpretive theological locus, which is grounded in the event character of Christ's self-revelation, so too election plays a similar role in Calvin's thought. Predestination names for Calvin that theologically rich manner by which God's gracious response to human sin cannot be seen to undo the justice of God, since God in Christ elects us freely for the sake of God's glory and our betterment. We consider now the manner in which these themes mutually re-enforce one another and sketch the contours of the doctrine of election.

As a student of Augustine, Calvin affirms sin as the condition which marks the human as justly deserving of damnation. Moreover, the deserts of sin are the human's and cannot be understood as a punishment serving as a payment which credits the debt of sin. Calvin sketches this out in terms of God's design in creation and redemption. God is identified as the author of all things, including human capacity and activity as evil.[33] The importance of this affirmation lay in Calvin's assertion that all that occurs is ordered to the glory of God, of which God alone can be responsible. The fall as such is described as predestined, because through even this dreadful decree the glory of God ultimately shines.[34] Yet Calvin carefully circumscribes this *theologoumenon* by asserting that sin "takes its occasion from man himself."[35] He describes human evil intention as the evident cause of sin and thereby suggests that human agency is not inactive in the fall from perfection. Humans are not off the hook even though God has authored the drama of creation and redemption in such a way as to include the fall of humans from their intended purpose. Of course, this raises the question regarding the justice of such a state of affairs.

Calvin asserts that the identity of God as the author of evil, a point picked up by Schleiermacher in *Christian Faith*, does not compromise God's justice. Calvin identifies the just as that which glorifies God by undermining any attempts to posit the possibility of an extra-theological canon by which God can be judged; nothing can precede God's will as a cause.[36] In point of fact, Calvin considers the inequality of grace as evidence that it is free.[37] As that which is truly free, grace then is founded in and ordered by God's freedom, which precludes not only the possibility of human credit but also subverts the assertion that grace denies God glory precisely in its discerning character. To assert the former of these two points is made possible only by utterly usurping the biblical witness in mistaking the effect of election for the cause of election. Election cannot be understood as a human credit because this would undermine the clearest expression of the grace of God as evidenced in the incarnation:

> Augustine wisely notes this: namely, that we have in the very Head of the church the clearest mirror of free election that we who are among the members may not be troubled about it; and that he was not made Son of God by righteous living but was freely given such honor so that he might afterward share his gift with others. If here anyone should ask why others were not as he was—or why all of us are separated from him by such a long distance—why all of us are corrupt, while he is purity itself, such a questioner would display not only his madness but with it also his shamelessness. But if they willfully strive to strip God of his free power to choose or reject, let them at the same time also take away what has been given to Christ.[38]

This strong christocentric formulation of election is also buttressed by Calvin's appeal to the manner in which redemption illumines parallels to election in creation itself. Gerrish notes that the mystery of predestination is congruent with the broad and evident mystery that is human existence itself.[39] This, in turn, is continuous with Calvin's strong affirmation of God's ordering of creation. That one human is elect rather than another is no stranger than the fact that a human is born a human rather than some other beast.[40] Calvin discovers in the illumination of revelation a continuity between creation and redemption that demonstrates a seeming capriciousness. That God has willed me to be a human and elect both reflect a sort of mystery that illustrates a human incapacity to know the mind of God. This incapacity is reflected in our discernment of the will of God as *secret*.[41] The inexplicability of election is a function of our finitude, as it were, and is wholly congruous with human nature as created. To ponder any other possibility is to usurp divine freedom by positing it as that which can be circumscribed by human ability, which would be the height of human arrogance and so the arrival of idolatry. The doctrine of predestination then affirms the divine design, which precludes human certitude based on the self and thrusts the believer into the grace of God, which is finally the pastoral intent of the doctrine.

Calvin understands, of course, that predestination can be differently received. He asserts that those who wrongly ponder election find themselves in a labyrinth without escape.[42] Those who rightly receive the doctrine, however, are recipients of its benefits. Included in that reception is the sure effect of being goaded into a life of holiness.[43] For this reason, predestination cannot be viewed as a deterrent to ethical behavior but is its very foundation insofar as believers are now secure in respect of their relationship with God and freed to further their relationship with the neighbor. Calvin admits the possibility of a kind of certainty that accompanies election. This certainty has an objective foundation in the fact that our perseverance is grounded in Christ's prayer for our salvation, which in turn elicits that subjective sense of an inner call that cannot deceive by virtue of the power of the preached word and the Spirit's illumination.[44] The believer is pressed to content herself with the promises of God that result from God's electing call of the individual. To query why this one rather than that one is elect is to broach the divine-human boundary marked by sovereignty, already evident in God's decision to choose Israel rather than other nations. Election is a part of the pattern of God's interaction with humans, although Calvin also notes a New Testament particularity in asserting the possibility of a kind of certainty afforded elect individuals, which cannot be accorded an elect *nation* since the former rather than the latter experience election in concert with regeneration.[45] Despite this discontinuity between election in the two testaments, there is the continuity recognizing that election is congruous with reprobation.[46] To be chosen is to be chosen from the midst of a community that is not chosen. This affirmation is that darkest of decrees in the thought of Calvin, which Schleiermacher takes up and creatively appropriates in a manner consonant with both his affirmation of the Reformed tradition and his desire to point to the significance of the doctrine of election within the context of a church union struggling to respect diversity while affirming the unity intended for the church by its Lord.

SCHLEIERMACHER ON ELECTION

Bretschneider, the Union Church, and Election

Schleiermacher alludes to Karl Gottlieb Bretschneider as that "famous theologian" whose *Aphorisms*[47] occasion his spirited defense of the Augustinian/Calvinian doctrine of election. Although this description might now strike us as tongue in cheek, it was not without some truth in Schleiermacher's day. Bretschneider, a Lutheran, was known in his day as a theologian engaged in attempting to resolve the competing attentions of supernaturalism and rationalism.[48]

Bretschneider was born on February 11, 1776, to a celebrated preacher and his wife who was a daughter of a pastor. Bretschneider describes his vocation as a theologian as an "accidental consequence" resulting from his father's wish and the fact that his mother's brothers were all theologians.[49] It is noted that his theological career was nearly aborted by his fall from orthodoxy, yet his observation that many respectable theologians were moving beyond the received tradition buoyed his hope, and so he took his theological exams in Dresden. He went on to further academic work and habilitated in spring 1804. The war of 1806 resulted in his exchanging an academic for an ecclesiastical career. He achieved some success in this, eventually becoming Superintendent in Annaberg in 1808. In 1809 he defended his dissertation on Josephus and seven years after began to serve as General Superintendent in Gotha and served in this capacity until his death in 1848.

Bretschneider was known for his frank defense of the need to guard freedom of thought and teaching in the face of the union of the protestant confessions.[50] This concern is evidenced in his *Aphorisms*. At the heart of his exposition of the matters to be addressed is the importance of carving a space for a straightforward treatment of points of difference. Indeed, Bretschneider holds there that it is only by a clear articulation of the differences of the teachings of the church that a union can be forged in some fashion.[51] In thinking through the differences between the Lutheran and Reformed confessions, Bretschneider is especially attentive to the Lutheran assertion of a real presence in the Eucharist and the Reformed treatment of election. He also notes that these distinctive features are often lost in the lives of parishes.[52] Yet Bretschneider finally comes to the conclusion that not all distinctive features are equal in significance. He sees in the Reformed treatment of election consequences that are injurious for the life of the church, and for this reason he critiques the Reformed treatment of election in the *Aphorisms*. He does so for the sake of the union church, for which he is in favor, granted that its external expression reflects an inner harmony between the two churches that is free and not forced.[53]

Bretschneider affirms points of agreement between the two confessions: Both affirm that God creates humans for moral good, despite the fall; that Jesus was sent to free humans from damnation and for eternal life; and that one is unable to better oneself because of original sin, for which reason faith is advanced as the means of our redemption.[54] The points of difference are no less clear. Lutherans believe that God's will is that all be saved, but that this will is conditioned by human acceptance or rejection of grace, which God foreknows. By contrast, the Reformed view is such that the human is unable to frustrate the will of God, and the fact of human salvation and damnation simply exists as a consequence of this will. This latter is unacceptable to Bretschneider, who asserts that there is no scriptural support for the Calvinian position.[55]

Bretschneider believes that election points first to God's choice with respect to Jesus and the apostles and secondly with respect to individual Christians. This latter presumes an election to salvation yet not damnation, and it does not presuppose the treatment of perseverance so dear to Reformed dogmatics.[56] Yet it must not be supposed that Bretschneider's problems are with the Reformed doctrine alone. He also critiques Lutheranism for so focusing on human enmity with God as to ignore that patent ability to will well as demonstrated in Paul's tortured expression that "I find it to be a law that when I want to do what is good, evil lies close at hand."[57] Here, Bretschneider draws near to Pelagianism in his assertion that the human is able in some fashion to effect her salvation by choosing well. He sees this as the necessary consequence of the biblical commendations to live morally; and while he affirms the systemic integrity of Reformed theology, he asserts that finally on account of its doctrine of election it renders ethics meaningless.[58] The practical consequences of the Calvinian doctrine of election, then, finally recommend its disavowal.[59] He notes as well that the Lutherans also need to distance themselves from their treatment of real presence in the Eucharist. Both doctrines fail with respect to scriptural integrity and rational acceptability, a point lost on those authoring the union. Bretschneider is finally in favor of the union—if it advances correctly—and sees it as the opportunity to clarify these issues.[60]

Scripture, Reason, and a Case for the Strict Formulation

In an observation that parallels Bretschneider's, Schleiermacher notes toward the end of the essay *On the Doctrine of Election* that the state of affairs in the emerging Union Church reflects a curious coming to terms— in which Lutherans are adopting the Calvinian view of the Lord's Supper at the same time as the Reformed are abandoning the Calvinian doctrine of predestination in favor of the Lutheran view (see p. 79 below). In keeping with Schleiermacher's irenic posture toward contentious issues, he recognizes the need for an *apologia* for his insistence on a return to the formula as he understands it in its Augustinian guise. In effect the treatise as a whole is this *apologia*. Throughout his construal of the Augustinian treatment of the doctrine of predestination Schleiermacher traces what he deems to be the graced character of salvation, a point shared by all. In Schleiermacher's estimation, anti-Pelagian and anti-Manichaean emphases mark the contours of this received tradition. The former underscores the inadmissibility of any precondition for redemption apart from God's unmerited grace. The latter points to the need to consider the significance of the fact that it is the predestining God who is subject of both creation and redemption and who acts in an utterly congruous character on both accounts. We will attend to these emphases of the strict formulation in considering Schleiermacher's response to Bretschneider.

At the heart of Bretschneider's critique of the Calvinian treatment of predestination is what he considers to be a deficient view of both Scripture and reason. Both of these critiques are answered by Schleiermacher who makes the case that the strict formulation, as found in Augustine's work, best reflects a theology attentive to the primary trajectory of the Christian story. For this reason Schleiermacher proposes that how one reads Scripture is necessarily informed by one's doctrinal commitments (see p. 45 below). Hence, the possibility of reading Scripture "objectively" is dismissed. This is why Schleiermacher prefaces his critique of the standard scriptural objections raised by Lutherans to the Reformed treatment of predestination with an analysis of the dogmatic potency of the strict formulation. We will briefly review the salient features of this important prolegomenon before attending to Schleiermacher's treatment of Scripture on predestination.

In outlining the significance of the strict formulation in preparation for answering critiques of it, Schleiermacher underscores the relationship of the doctrine of election to practical Christianity and the historical character of God's dealing with the world. In outlining the practical significance of the Reformed doctrine of election he anticipates the stock critique of the ethical quandary resulting from a notion of double predestination: if one is predestined to salvation, or not, it matters not what one does since one's future is sealed. Consequently, human nature tends toward vice rather than virtue. Schleiermacher responds that Calvin is well aware of the dual dangers of pride and complacency resulting from a confidence in one's salvation, as well as despair resulting from uncertainty regarding one's salvation. He notes that the source of Bretschneider's confusion on this issue results from an unwillingness to entertain what Calvin asserts: that "the pious life and blessedness are one and the same" (p. 38). Consequently, insofar as the pious walk by faith, their walk is informed by the redemption in which they participate and by which the Spirit lives and works in the redeemed. Moreover, Schleiermacher observes that this doctrine itself asserts this latter point and thereby serves to point to the only way by which morality can be achieved in the life of the faithful. Of some consequence, here, is Schleiermacher's clear conviction that doctrine not only shapes how we read Scripture but also how we live our lives. For that reason, in his defense of Calvin's position he draws attention to the importance of the theme of the preserving power of grace that is a mark of the strict formulation.[61] This teaching alone suffices to mitigate the paralyzing consequences of despair occasioned by the belief in the possibility of the forfeiture of grace, the very weakness marking the Lutheran position (p. 39).

As one would expect from a Reformed theologian, treating the practical consequences of a dogmatic locus has important bearings on the task of proclamation, which appears as a topic at some critical junctures. Schleiermacher asserts that it is the hearing of the gospel that serves to suspend the contempt of God that is a distinctive mark of being human apart from redemption (p. 27). He recognizes, of course, that it is not the Reformed church alone that asserts the importance of proclamation for this transformative event. The Reformed church shares with the Lutheran confession a high estimation of preaching as the locus for the granting of faith (p. 60). Predestination is, in effect, that which makes possible a hearing of the Word since it is by predestination that God disposes one, or not, to "the pious feelings that the Spirit effects through the Word" (p. 29). For this reason, it is not too surprising that Schleiermacher notes that the aim of Calvin's preaching is to point his hearer to the reality of her incapacity, as illumined by the Spirit, so that this same hearer is thereby inspired to seek divine wisdom from Scripture and one's own experience (p. 41). His interest in relating the doctrine of predestination with the kerygmatic practice set the practical significance of the doctrine of election squarely within the praxis of the church, which is understood with an eye to its historical location.

A determinative concern rehearsed by Schleiermacher throughout this monograph is his assessment of the importance of considering the historical character of God's working. He writes that "one can never refer to something that God has only foreseen but not previously provided for."[62] Moreover, he considers this theme to be decisive for correctly understanding the Augustinian position, the very proposition that Bretschneider considers to ground the ethical quandary he critiques, as was noted above.[63] The notion that God provides for that which will be foreseen signals God's attention to the details through which God works and marks the historical as the means created by God and engaged in the eternal decree of election. This posits the importance of understanding the historical as the arena for the eternal act of God, and it thereby establishes God's ordination as the *sine qua non* for understanding the manner of the working of God in history. This, in effect, sets a determinative theological agenda that enables Schleiermacher to respond to critiques of the strict formulation on the basis of particular passages in Scripture.

In considering Bretschneider's critiques, Schleiermacher is especially attentive to the question regarding the universality of the will of God for redemption. In addressing this first question in preparation for a response to Bretschneider's critique of the Calvinian use of Scripture, Schleiermacher appeals to the letter to the Romans to introduce a point that he will clarify later in the work. He observes that God does not intend decrees for particular persons but rather for humanity as such. This is an important theme for considering the Romans 5 passage with its allusions to the universal character of the gift of salvation in verse 15. He asserts that the ebb and flow of the development of the human race in God's act of redeeming it inevitably entails the rejection of some concurrent with the redemption of others, the very point asserted by Paul in Romans insofar as the rejection of the gospel by the Jews occasioned the inclusion of the Gentiles. This point, Schleiermacher contends, needs to be kept in mind in considering the broader Lutheran critique of the Calvinian treatment of the universality of salvation. It is for that reason, to cite 1 Timothy 2:4 as an example, that the word "all" need not be understood literally (p. 46). This is demonstrated in that the word "all" in another example (Titus 2:11) cannot be understood literally since Christ did not literally appear to all people. "All" is a qualified adjective in Scripture. For this reason, Bretschneider is mistaken when he asserts that the Lutheran church is more faithful to Scripture when it asserts the universal will of God's redemption, which is betrayed by Lutheranism's own admission that not all are saved (p. 48). For Schleiermacher, the word "all" points to the omnipotent potentiality of the power of redemption and not its actuality: "all" simply reminds us that God's redemptive power can never be exhausted (p. 48).

Schleiermacher considers Bretschneider's critique of the strict formulation as incongruent with the potentials of reason to be disingenuous. Moreover, Bretschneider's estimation of reason, as that which is able to penetrate the depths of the mystery of the divine decree (p. 70), expects too much of reason. Bretschneider, Schleiermacher notes, fails to discern the aporetic character of reason's path. If reason regularly fails to discern the whys and wherefores of creation, how can one expect it to plumb the depths of the oracles of God? (p. 70). The problem, Schleiermacher argues, is one of confusing categories. Reason is only able to ponder the path of effective causes. But history and religion are dependent on a final cause, which is beyond the reach of reason. In effect reason merely, although significantly, demonstrates the limit that inexorably draws it to its point of impenetrability. In a sense, however, reason participates in the beyond of this limit by its vague awareness of the interconnection of all that is and the manner in which this all is cast upon the providence of God. Yet, even this latter awareness operates only at the level of the general, and particular questions regarding why one person is redeemed, yet not the other, escape the capacity of reason. Reason attempts to grasp that totality, which contains it and is, in fact, communicated to it in glimpses by the Reign of God (p. 75).

Creation, Redemption, and the Singular Decree

From the outset, it needs to be affirmed that Schleiermacher contends that the ways in which God works in both creation and redemption are congruous.[64] Throughout the document, Schleiermacher holds forth the conditions of creation as demonstrative of the manner in which God works redemption. And so, for example, he contends that the Lutheran willingness to admit the damnation of sinners who die before experiencing a *kairotic* moment simply does not differ in kind from the doctrinal assertion that the reprobate are ordained to damnation. Since God works in time, God's refusal to act in one way is itself an action of God. For this reason, the Lutheran notion of divine permission as a way to explain evil is a ruse. In effect, Schleiermacher considers God to be the author of sin and evil, since this is consequent to the notion that God is the final cause of all that is.[65] He notes that the only way to avoid this notion would be to consider evil a nonreality, which would merely utterly collapse the possibility of distinguishing God's permission and ordination, which is foundational for the Lutheran position (pp. 69, 70).

At the heart of Schleiermacher's treatment of election is his insistence on the singularity of the divine decree. This oft-repeated assertion trades on the notion that the long-standing philosophical paradox of the one and the all is finally resolved in the plenitude of that unity which holds all in singularity by the divine author of all that is. As Schleiermacher notes, how can one

> say of God that for God the universal and the particular are different objects, are they then to be understood as objects of cognition or of willing? That is to say, it is indeed only because of the imperfections of our knowledge that for us the oneness of what is universal is different from the totality of what is particular and our knowledge is so much the more genuine and lively the more the two merge together. (p. 55)

This very important passage may provide us with some perspective from which to resolve the seeming insolubility of the notion that God speaks singularly in respect of the intent of creation, and the biblical assertion that God in Christ is entrenched in time and necessarily described narratively. Is Schleiermacher's God so wholly other in uttering all that was, is, and will be so as to be unassailably singular? Is there room to imagine mutuality in God and in God's relationship with humanity? It seems that the above quotation leads us to see that the particular and the universal are not merely resolved in the singularity of the decree of God, but, more importantly, this singularity does not collapse the importance of narrating God's dealing with humans. Neither does such a view necessarily deprive one of imagining a triune identity of God, but instead it impels us to consider that our inability to think of plurality and singularity simultaneously merely points us to the fragmented character of knowing. As we ponder the seemingly arbitrary character of God's acts of creation and redemption, we assert that the singularity of the divine decree orders God's apparently incomprehensible acts to God's all-embracing plan for redemption. More importantly, however, knowing the singularity of the divine decree enables us better to divine that this act of God here and that act of God there have integrity as a part, and perhaps as a partner, in the greater whole.

At first blush, one might imagine Schleiermacher to have a rather flat view of history; perhaps as evolving under the aegis of the singular decree or as a bland manifestation of the entelechy that such a singularity entails. But this essay develops a wholly alternate view. The singularity of the decree is, in its appearance in history, demonstrably marked by ebb and flow, expansion and contraction, and the conflict these entail (cf. p. 44). Moreover, it is precisely in this give-and-take of history that we find the locus for God's advance preparation.[66] Our apprehension of God's action as temporal and so contingent, however, does not gainsay the essentially eternal foundation and the consequent singularity of God's decree. Our apprehension of this decree is to be framed by the theological affirmation that God's will is God's justice, which does not admit an external canon by which to judge this singular decree in its plenitude (p. 65). This theme of singularity, by which we understand the nature of God's will, is of utmost import for this treatise and resurfaces in Schleiermacher's treatment of the human in the modes of redemption and condemnation.

Election and Human Solidarity

Wholly integrated with the theme of the singularity of the divine decree, is Schleiermacher's insistence that humanity also needs to be considered in its singularity, a rather counterintuitive move at the inception of the modern period. Yet, this is a theme consistently underlined by Schleiermacher, and it is also evident in his *Glaubenslehre*.[67] It contains two key sub-themes that need to be understood in order to discern Schleiermacher's assessment of the utility of the strict formulation for pastoral counsel.

First, Schleiermacher's treatment of the singularity of the human condition in relationship to each individual person is consonant with the relationship he envisions between the singular decree and the historical ebb and flow that comprises the material of our experience. Individuality, like history, is parasitic on its foundation, the singularity of humanity for the individual and the singularity of the divine decree for history.[68] Consequently, the notion of "humanity" is not an erasure of individuality but is the very condition for its possibility and the *telos* of the appearance of the individual. This appearance itself is ingeniously explicated by Schleiermacher in that the individual is properly a predicate of the redeemed person. In speaking of the relationship of the notion of the corporate person to the individual, he writes, "in the religious sense, however, they are not yet persons but first become such through rebirth when the Holy Spirit will have brought about faith in them. On account of this process, this very transformation is called 'regeneration' because in this sphere it is the beginning of one's own individual life of freedom" (p. 64).

Second, elsewhere Schleiermacher speaks of the "mass of humanity," a singular and undifferentiated potentiality that has not received the identity that constitutes redemption. In a sense, this phenomenology of redemption points to the mass from which the individual is drawn and constituted as the individual. The singularity of the decree that effects this constitution means that the call of God constitutes both election and rejection whereby "the human race is to be transformed into the spiritual body of Christ" (p. 76). Yet, it might seem as if this very description invites one to consider redemption as a bifurcation of humanity. This, however, is not the case insofar as Schleiermacher augments this image with his emphasis on the simultaneity of the levels of human existence as necessary to the completion of the human race.

In this respect, Schleiermacher presupposes the notion of "levels" of humanity as he argues against Bretschneider's claim that to consider God's decision to elect one and not the other is wholly arbitrary. He notes that one can respond to such a claim only with one of two alternatives: either we switch around who is redeemed and who is not, a solution that is no solution at all; or we posit that God has created all on an equal footing, and their redemption is deemed to be their choice. This proposal, Schleiermacher argues, also fails as a solution since the cause for the redemption of one and the condemnation of the other is located in the fiat of the human and is thus thoroughly arbitrary. For Schleiermacher, the real solution to the problem lay in two related assertions: First, insofar as God's will cannot be subject to an external canon, the will of God is beyond reproach and cannot be deemed arbitrary. Second, the notion of humans as existing at different levels trades on something of an evolutionary view of humanity as a singularity.[69] The push and pull, the extension and contraction that constitute the development of every physical reality also constitute the development of humankind. And so Schleiermacher writes,

> However, it also follows, in part, that because damnation is taken to be a necessary stage, it must also be a stage of development, for in the domain of active spiritual nature the two cannot be separated. It also follows, in part, that the damned likewise cannot be excluded from being objects of the divine love since everything that belongs to the ordered world of human life must be an object of the divine attributes. (pp. 77, 78)

Schleiermacher thus hints at a christologically ordered universalism insofar as these stages of development are necessarily temporal.[70] Consequently, when human development has reached its *telos*, and the human race is the body of Christ, these differentiated human levels will have been resolved as the plenitude of humanity existent as the singularity of the body of Christ, joined to the head.[71] Moreover, this image of the *anakephalaiōsasthai*[72] of all alone resolves the problem posed in the realization that the beatitude of eternal redemption would be sorely compromised by the realization that our beloved who are not redeemed suffer the eternal haunts of hell. In Schleiermacher's estimation, this very theme is best advanced by the strict formulation, despite the failure of its early advocates to promote it.

In sum, Schleiermacher makes the case that the strict formulation best counters the Pelagian and Manichaean dangers inherent in thinking through the notion of election. Moreover, this is the case because the strict formulation best explicates Scripture, makes the most sense of the role of reason and history, and clearly advances what Schleiermacher takes to be axiomatic, namely, the role of the singular as a way to understand the decree of God and the constitution of the human. Moreover, the strict formulation, in Schleiermacher's version, provides for pastoral counsel on many fronts, including the grounding of a christological ethic and providing comfort in light of the eternal state of humanity.

Election, Dogmatics, and the Task of Theology

Matthias Gockel wrote of the inattention Schleiermacher's essay *On the Doctrine of Election* receives as over against what it deserves.[73] This may be a comment, not so much on the lost nature of this seminal document for the thought of Schleiermacher, as Gockel convincingly demonstrates, but rather on the lost nature of the dogmatic utility of the doctrine of election. One rarely finds theological monographs dedicated to this locus that clearly captivated significant attention in Schleiermacher's time. Likewise, election seems to fail to arrest the imaginations of theologians today. Or, perhaps, seemingly more pressing items at hand demand theological attention.

Karl Barth was, of course, the significant exception to this observation.[74] The second half of his second volume of *Church Dogmatics* carefully exegetes this doctrine and its significance for the life of the church.[75] The points of emphasis are well known but bear repetition.[76] Jesus Christ is the singular instance of the union of the electing God and the elected human.[77] This christological font for thinking about election demands that general principles cannot be a maxim by which we understand the drama of election, which is, in fact, an event in the freedom of God.[78] Consequently, Barth views the divine decision to be incarnate as constitutive of the divine essence.[79] Moreover, this freedom of God is precisely a freedom by God to be rejected for our sake.[80] Our experiences of both election and rejection, then, are derivative.[81] Barth, in effect, provides us with a new vantage point from which to ponder the significance of election. The only question that remains is this: why has so little come of this fertile ground? Why has Barth come to share in Schleiermacher's fate of receiving so little reaction to such provocative thought? Undoubtedly, disinterest in both treatments reflects, in part, a general reception of some variation of universalism. Election as a resolution of the question regarding the salvation of humankind is of little concern when we are under no anxiety concerning that question. Yet, this diagnosis is probably too facile in that there is more at stake than universalism resolves. Disinterest in the question of election demonstrates a contemporary distance from something that both Schleiermacher and Barth and their theological forebears were passionate about.

Election is decidedly about God's choice. As a dogmatic locus, it points our attention unreservedly toward God as the agent of choice in the drama of salvation. In the wake of the terrors that have shaped modernity this emphasis is sometimes considered suspect for ethics, since it might be deemed to elicit quietism and fatalism. Yet Schleiermacher asserts in this monograph that this critique simply will not do. God elects to redeem, and redemption effects a change. God's election does not render the human agent a patient but instead makes an agent of the patient. Finally, Schleiermacher, like many of his interlocutors, sees election as a corollary of the doctrine of justification. Election is about the divine declaration that transforms the individual human as well as humanity.

Unlike many heirs of modernity Schleiermacher refuses to think of the individual in abstraction from humanity, especially in his treatment of election. The taxonomy of choice in the parlance of Schleiermacher is that God chooses human community on which our individuality is staked. This is far removed from modern sensibilities in which I first choose God, then choose to locate that relationship within a community, or not, and if the former, I choose which community that will be. It is Schleiermacher's emphasis on election as the action of God which might be decidedly uncomfortable for many moderns insofar as we continue to render choice as the instantiation of the subject and hesitate to respond to the clarion call of the Reformation, inviting us to render to God the most important and precious of all things: choice itself.

ON THE DOCTRINE OF ELECTION, WITH SPECIAL REFERENCE TO THE *APHORISMS* OF DR. BRETSCHNEIDER

ELECTION: FROM CONTROVERSY TO CONSOLATION

For quite some time people have customarily designated the strict formulation of this doctrine by the formula "the unconditional divine decree." As is well known, the formulation was first expounded by Augustine and finally by Calvin. Both did this in two respects. On the one hand, they felt driven by the clearest declarations of scripture to put the doctrine in this way and not otherwise. On the other hand, they also showed how contradictions to the purest rational notions regarding the divine being would necessarily arise if one were to deviate from this strict formulation. Yet, only in a comparatively small portion of the Christian church had this formulation produced a lasting conviction. In contrast, after various and sundry battles it was rejected by the greatest portion of the church and indeed on each occasion precisely because this formulation contradicted both the clear declarations of scripture and just as obviously contradicted sound reason.

Ever since I have been in a position to occupy myself with such a topic I have been astonished with this result in that I found no one on the opposing side who had demonstrated a more unbounded reverence for scripture than these two men. In fact, I would not even wish to grant the great Luther precedence over Calvin in this matter, for even where they differ from each other in their interpretation of scripture the one is as firmly committed to scripture as the other, and where differences between them do exist it is simply a matter of their different ways of reconciling apparently contradictory statements. Just as little would I want to maintain that any of the determined opponents of that view has surpassed the godly Augustine and the pious Calvin in the rigor of the ordering of their thoughts. Moreover, it seemed to me unlikely that their assertions could have stood in clear contradiction to other general truths and also to these truths that Augustine and Calvin themselves acknowledged, truths that those men themselves would not have noted but which would first have had to be pointed out to them by their opponents.

Nor was I ever able to understand the frequently repeated excuse that it was an excessive zeal in his controversy with Pelagius that first enticed the godly Augustine into adopting this view which supposedly contradicts both reason and scripture, and that Calvin too belongs in this succession as one of the last in the chain, whereas on the other hand, Luther and his followers had fortunately removed themselves from the trap. Since it had never seemed to me to be the case that, for Augustine, this doctrine first emerged in the midst of and as a result of the controversy but that it belonged entirely and essentially among the original convictions which summoned him to participate in it and which inspired him throughout the conflict, I should be surprised if the new historical and critical studies of this controversy and of the entire period during which it was conducted, studies that we can anticipate from two excellent men, should fail to shed the clearest possible light on this very matter.[1]

Now, with regard to Calvin: he is indeed so undeniably a disciple of Augustine as only a distinguished man can ever be called the disciple of another. However, his very agreement with his teacher in this matter certainly did not arise in any polemical way, for much less prevalent in his writings than in those of the other Reformers is the point of view that the disputed statements of the Roman church are to be traced back to Pelagianism. Rather, Calvin's conviction with regard to this matter was as original to him as any that he ever held. Thus, to both men that defense[2] seems to have proved quite useless. Moreover, I have always regretted that it was so readily attributed to them, certainly very much against their own wish and will. That is to say, were one to be as vigorously convinced, as I am, that this doctrine was neither developed in controversy by the one nor merely learned and repeated by the other but for both was an original truth and essential component of their Christian faith, then one would surely have had more reservations about so repeatedly and readily declaring it contrary to reason and scripture. Indeed, when I considered the way in which this doctrine, which admittedly was at first woven into Augustine's great controversy with Pelagius, in no respect prevented the doctrine of the former from becoming the system of the Western church, which was constantly compelled to secure stricter cohesion and firmer unity within its body of doctrine, and when I consider the way in which this particular point was first rejected only in a later development, then it will always seem to me that if only Augustine himself had been able to remedy what he said at that time or if his later disciple (i.e. Gottschalk) had presented it entirely in his spirit and in the right context, it would have been upheld in honor and respect for even much longer. Moreover, Gottschalk[3] was no more an Augustine than were the later defenders of Calvin against the attacks of the Arminians, who were inspired by none other than Gottschalk himself.

It is on this account that I have never presumed to agree with the greatest majority of contemporaries in their condemnation of the teaching of those men as contrary to reason and scripture. However, the form taken by the doctrine that replaced it did not appear to me to be satisfactory either, because, on the one hand, it seemed to me to tend to lead one around in circles, and on the other hand, to the extent that one can confidently, unwaveringly focus one's attention on it, instead of offering a definite and clear notion, it presented only negations and restrictions instead. Therefore, it appeared to me all the more that it was not conceived originally but rather was more the product of controversy, also that it suffered from those uncertainties and deficiencies which tend to be characteristic of opinions that arise in this way. Hence, for this reason I was sorry to find that the controversy about this subject seemed as though it had fallen asleep, and it was my ardent wish that the matter might somehow be explicated anew so as to determine whether perhaps the topic could be sorted out clearly and fully in a fourth attempt instead of leaving it forgotten and abandoned as has been done hitherto and as seemed to me to have prevailed among the theological public, and so as to determine whether, after renewed fermentation in a fourth round, a fully clarified conviction might finally come about.

Finally, since the most recent efforts toward church union, which naturally must again have called to mind the points debated between the two parties, this wish is beginning to be fulfilled. Moreover, with my claim that this controversy belongs more to the academy than to life and that no consideration should be given to these opposing opinions with regard to the ordering of relationships within the church, unintentionally enough I myself have assisted in giving these efforts a push, one that at least has not remained entirely unsuccessful if indeed Dr. Bretschneider's *Aphorisms* also unquestionably relate to what I have said partly with regard to my opinion of the controversy itself and partly with regard to the justification of our proceedings in connection with the already initiated union of the two churches. However, if my wishes are to be yet further fulfilled, many more aspects of the matter will still have to be clarified, more so than has been the case until now. Moreover, since my expectation that there would also surely arise a defender of the original Calvinian, or rather Augustinian, doctrine is all but disappointed, I would no longer restrain myself but would take up this opportunity as occasioned by the presentation of the famous theologian just named, not intending in any way to enter into any controversy with a man whose learning and excellent merit I acknowledge as does any other, and who moreover is committed in as lively a way as I am to the wish for the union of the two separated church parties. Nor do I intend to earn or to justify any reputation of being a bold and determined disciple of Calvin which might be thought proper to confer on me—though for reasons unknown to me. Rather, I simply want to draw attention to those points that also in the conduct of the present dispute against Calvin seem to me to have in part been overlooked and in part not considered with the attention that is properly due to them.

In this latter category there belongs, above all, precisely that with which Dr. Bretschneider begins by bringing into view the relationship of the two theories of election to the rest of the theological system. What is admitted is this, that in the system of the Lutheran church itself, there is a doctrinal proposition[4] that contradicts the Lutheran theory of election, namely, a proposition asserting the complete incapacity of human beings to better themselves and asserting their natural resistance to divine grace through which alone they receive power to do so. However, as he acknowledges, the Calvinian theory is in closest agreement with this doctrine. Now, with this I too am in complete agreement: that in these contrasting ways both theories of election relate to that doctrine of the indispensability of divine grace in connection with the conversion of human beings, and I have always felt that this is really that axis on which the whole controversy turns. Nevertheless, this point is not always stressed as relevant to the matter but is rather placed in the shadows and presented by some as though that doctrine of grace is equally compatible with both theories of election. Hence, the unfettered openness with which *Aphorisms* acknowledges this point cannot receive sufficient praise. Accordingly, it thus appears to be a matter of choice whether one acknowledges the indispensability of divine grace for sanctification yet then also wishes to endure the strict Calvinian formula regarding election, or whether one avoids this point and its consequences by means of the Lutheran formula but thereby also dispenses with the necessity of divine grace and so seeks to stand on one's own two feet.

Now, Dr. Bretschneider very resolutely and quickly makes up his mind about the choice that confronts him and affirms that since one cannot locate it in scripture the theologian must abandon that premise without hesitation precisely because the Calvinian theory strictly and necessarily follows from it. He adheres to those passages in scripture from which one can conclude that even without divine grace the human being is capable of doing what is good even though one is not always able to achieve it fully. This is so, he says, for even though one also does not succeed in achieving the good fully even with divine grace, yet at least in willing it (purely and radically?) one is also able to fear God and to do what is right apart from any relationship to Christ, and in that one rejects that Calvinian premise in this way one also avoids the Calvinian doctrine of predestination, and, according to Dr. Bretschneider's view, all its so very serious consequences.

LUTHER AND THE LUTHERANS ON ELECTION

However, it is surely not to be believed that all theologians of the Lutheran church will be quite so resolute. This is so, for many will certainly say that where Paul describes the initial willing of what is good he portrays it as a mere wishing, as empty and impotent desire, as an unsatisfied longing, for he also describes it as being impossible wholly to fulfill. The human being in this condition is portrayed as a person who yearns to be delivered from "this body of death."[5] Moreover, when Peter in amazement proclaims that any person, even among the heathen, "who fears God and does what is right is acceptable to God"[6] he does not mean thereby that such a one is in and of oneself acceptable to God but acceptable in the sense that the gospel should be preached to such a person. It is precisely these theologians who will hold to those other passages which imply that we are what we are "through grace,"[7] that the human being must be "born of the Spirit,"[8] that Christ alone can deliver one from that body of death,[9] that salvation is to be found neither in the law nor in human nature in and of itself but only in Christ. Precisely these theologians, then, will attest that they need something other than that natural capacity, something more than that which is referred to in scripture as that knowledge of the moral law that is also attributed to the heathen and that capacity to resist disobedience to it on account of which they can be found punishable, and so their faith is that it is precisely God through Christ who offers this additional gift[10] to human beings, something that they can never attain through natural means. Now, if Dr. Bretschneider's affirmation is correct, all these theologians would have to ally themselves with the Calvinian theory because the Lutheran theory, if it is not to appear inconsistent, demands too costly a sacrifice of their faith. In short, all those who attribute an exclusive value to redemption through Christ and to the operations of grace that proceed from his Spirit, all those theologians who cling to these distinctive inner experiences[11] of Christians will rather agree to endure the Calvinian theory that Christ was sent by God for the purpose of truly redeeming at least a portion from among all who are in need of redemption rather than to fulfill the claim that he was sent for all and his redemption extends to all, or, if this latter should prove incompatible with the first theory, to adopt another theory from which it would follow in the end that Christ was sent for all, but needlessly, if human beings were able to aid and abet themselves, and, as it were, to lift themselves out of the morass by the scruff of their own necks.

Now, this is an implication which has not very often been properly taken into consideration, and Dr. Bretschneider has surely gained much credit for his new and thorough treatment of the matter and for having exposed it impartially and without compromise. What has repeatedly been brought to light is that the Calvinian theory is detrimental to the universality of redemption and that the Lutheran theory confirms it. However, the fact that the Calvinian theory confirms the necessity of redemption and that the Lutheran theory impairs it is a matter that is seldom openly admitted by the defenders of the Lutheran theory. Yet, there are many who will not grant Dr. Bretschneider even this, for when Luther and Melanchthon depart from the stricter mode of presenting the divine decree they would necessarily have been mistaken and not handled it consistently in that in this respect it certainly did not occur to them to abandon this one tenet in their system concerning the natural incapacity of the human being for sanctification,[12] and the Lutheran church must have been completely mistaken in wanting to place the Solid Declaration in which the Calvinian theory of gracious election[13] is to some extent dealt with as a matter of controversy alongside the Augsburg Confession and its Apology in both of which an emphatic and rigorous polemic is directed against the Pelagian and semi-Pelagian view of the self-sufficiency of human beings. Instead, then, the *Book of Concord* was in fact discordant.[14] It was not excessive anti-Pelagian zeal on Augustine's part that led him to develop this theory. It is much rather the case that the entire basis of the controversy is lodged solely within the *Book of Concord* itself, and all great teachers commit an error when they view the anti-Pelagian Augsburg Confession as the safeguard of the Lutheran Church but reject out of hand Calvin's strict view of gracious election as a dangerous doctrine which can never be accepted. In contrast, I believe that the connection between these two doctrines is made clearer if we attend somewhat more closely to the statements of the Lutheran school than Dr. Bretschneider holds to be appropriate in this publication of his which he has designed for a wider circle.

The matter is precisely this: the theory of election of the Lutheran church asserts that God has ordained for blessedness those persons whom God foresaw would believe.[15] However, in this connection Article V of the Augsburg Confession teaches, "For by the Word . . . the Holy Spirit is given, who works faith when and where it pleases God, in those that hear the Gospel. . . ." [16] This means, then, that from eternity God ordained to blessedness those whom God foresaw would receive from the selfsame God the Holy Spirit, who works faith. Therefore, once one is committed to this claim, namely, to the fact that the Holy Spirit must work faith, the Calvinian formula again arises from the Lutheran formula in that for this effecting of faith the Augsburg Confession knows of no other principle than the same divine discretion "where and when it pleases God." Thus, it is easy to see how little the additional remark with regard to "hearing the Gospel" alters this fact. That is to say, insofar as this hearing is a self-initiated activity of the human being, faith does not depend on it, for faith is actually effected only "where and when it pleases God." Yet, that self-initiated activity is also certainly incompatible with the fact that to the human being in the condition of sin there is also attributed a "contempt of God,"[17] and all power to initiate any spiritual activity is denied to such persons, for hearing itself is certainly a suspension[18] of this contempt and as a self-initiated activity it is the beginning of spiritual activity. However, hearing is dependent upon proclamation and to the extent that God does not let the gospel be preached to all human beings, the Lutheran church[19] also considers this to be but the legitimate divine punishment for those sins which have nevertheless been committed by those to whom it has been preached. Moreover, when one inquires about the reason for the difference in treatment, no other can be found than once again that of the foreseen gift of faith. Furthermore, as Dr. Bretschneider states, it does indeed then follow from this finding that anyone who wants to have a consistent body of doctrine and who is committed to the view that the human being is completely incapable of any spiritual activity and that faith is effected through the Holy Spirit by means of the Word cannot escape the Calvinian theory. Yet it seems to me that in asserting that the Lutheran theologians would so easily give up that doctrine Dr. Bretschneider goes too far. On the contrary, I find the doctrine in all those textbooks that enjoy the widest respect, both in the older textbooks and in the most recent ones:

> "The original efficient cause of faith . . . is God, or the Holy Spirit, which is the same thing"[20]

And

> ". . . who . . . by the power of the Holy Spirit, began to believe in Christ."[21]

So, too,

> "The person who arbitrarily assumes . . . that in one's own present condition and nature one is in the position to initiate one's conversion or even to ask for it does so without any right notion of God or of human beings . . ."[22]

Likewise, de Wette[23] states that the advantage of the orthodox system on this point is clear. Indeed, what further instances should I add beyond these particular examples, which are most widely agreed upon and best known? It is rather the case that everything then depends upon how it is that so many pious and learned men have believed themselves able to reconcile the two opinions.

ELECTION AND THE NATURE OF FAITH

However, the help most familiar to us in this matter is this: faith certainly cannot arise other than through the inward working[24] of the Holy Spirit; however, on the part of the human being these influences[25] may or may not be resisted.[26] Let it be stated here in the words of a very highly respected theologian, a person who holds firmly to the doctrine of his church, in words that are chosen with great care and that are well calculated to leave the fewest possible openings through which the Calvinian theory can be penetrated.[27] He states that the divine Word, to the extent that it of course comprises the power of the divine Spirit and acts with it, inspires pious sensations,[28] and human beings can cherish these, nourish them, and follow them. This, he says, is the description of conversion, the beginning of which healing change is the subject matter of this paragraph. On the other hand, he indicates, a human being can also suppress and neglect these pious stirrings, and this is then the subtle description of resistance. He holds that one should think this slight beginning must be attributed to human freedom so that owing to this the human being is at that point the author of one's own harmful fate if one suppresses those stimuli, whereas God alone, from whom these first stirrings come, remains the author of one's propitious destiny if one does not resist them. Dr. Bretschneider must also have had this finest detail in mind but considered it inadmissible if indeed those pious sensations are to be ascribed to something other than the divine Spirit working through the divine Word. In this connection I am completely in agreement with his opinion, yet since one usually does regard this information as admissible it therefore seems to me that the matter calls for some further discussion.

Some, then, resist, or rather they neglect these pious sensations. Yet how does this come about? That same author directs our attention to the very tyranny of desire's resistance and in the same passage cited states, "The rise and the liveliness of those pious stirrings would be supported and defended against this strong power by divine help,"[29] and from these words it is not at all difficult to develop the entire Calvinian theory. This is so, for if it is divine help that prevents desire from squelching the onset of what is good, then precisely suppression or neglect will follow if the divine help is absent, and the divine help's being absent or not absent is precisely what divine predestination means. Anyone need only hold up as examples the different cases that can be thought of in this connection and the matter will not be left in any doubt. That is to say, suppose that I ask, if a person resists stimuli coming from the Spirit today, would this same person have likewise resisted these same stimuli at all times? Everyone will answer the question in the negative, because we know that desire is not always aroused to the same level of strength. Still, does it depend upon the human being whether or not stimuli from the Spirit come upon one today or at some other time? Moreover, is it not rather the case that this fortunate encounter of a strong stimulus with a weak resistance, whereby the former can take root and then indeed has so much strength that when a stronger resistance arises it can no longer be wholly suppressed, is not this precisely the divine help which can either be present or remain absent? Indeed, suppose that a human being possessed in oneself something that would come to the help of those stimuli, something that in no respect would itself be involved in the nature of desire! But that would have to be something more than the natural moral feeling, which is always cited in this connection—for this is always woven into the personal existence[30] of the civil society to which we belong and into the times in which we live as part of the sense of honor and public spirit of that time and place. With these things desire thus also has its sport[31]— hence that "something more" would have to be precisely that love for God, which the premise from which we have proceeded has denied to the natural human being and which certainly could of itself bring forth precisely those stirrings of the Spirit within us. However, if one does not have such a "something more," whether the Spirit neglects those stirrings then always ultimately depends simply on the condition of the desire in which the stirrings influenced by the Spirit encounter a person within.[32] Moreover, if one nevertheless says that one has this in one's power, one always makes the mistake of expecting something that is prior to faith and before conversion, when in fact it is received only with faith and through conversion; and indeed if that premise with which we started is valid, then this is something that one cannot give to oneself.

Now, suppose that we compare one person with another and try to find yet something else—other than that for the one person there has been a fortunate encounter of the stirrings aroused by the Spirit with divine help and for the other person none. Then certainly all that we can say is that some further reason for this is to be found in the human being. Accordingly, the desire in the one person must be altogether stronger than in the other person. Yet what is the basis of this difference? It is of course to be found in turn only in enticements that operate externally or in one's natural predisposition or in both together, and neither the one nor the other comes from the inner self of the individual person but rather comes to the person from God. Moreover, because the predispositions make up one's personal nature, and without the divine Spirit one can take advantage of external influences only in accordance with one's predispositions, it is precisely these two factors together that constitute divine predestination. This is true whether or not one comes to neglect and suppress the pious sensations[33] that the Spirit effects through the Word. Therefore, it is quite clear that from whichever point someone wants to trace something foreseen by God, it will always be something that the self-same God—if one should but trace it back far enough—has ordained through God's originating creative will.

Further, if we consider yet again the person who has cherished and nourished one's pious sensations and who has then been converted and if we ask whether it was precisely those first among the stirrings proceeding from the Spirit through the Word that this person cherished in this way, then of course this question cannot be answered in the affirmative in all cases. Nor, therefore, can one go on to assert that every person is converted at the first impact or not at all: rather one must assert that all confessions of every person whether they embrace or reject the operations of grace are, on that account, replete with admissions that even in their years of discernment and sound judgment they frequently rejected various summons toward what is good. Now, what is to be said of a person who, once having accepted the proffered divine grace prior to having then rejected it, were by some God-sent accident to have died? Or consider the case of two persons, one of whom has rejected the proffered grace and has then died—and ultimately we have to take note of this matter, for at least in their public teaching both parties maintain that the condition of a person in eternity is dependent upon one's situation at the moment of death—but the other person who has also rejected it but continues to live and is repeatedly addressed by that proffered grace until this person finally does not neglect or suppress it: is this not then the divine predestination that allots blessedness to the one and damnation to the other?[34] Is this not precisely what, having chiefly such a case in mind, Calvin himself calls a "dreadful decree"?[35] Is it not precisely what Calvin called "God's eternal decree, by which he compacted with himself what he willed to become of each man" (*Inst.* 3.21.5)? Suppose, moreover, that after one rejection or after repeated rejections by one person the summons continually recur, whereas another person finds oneself in a situation in which one is no longer addressed by these summons. Does it not then have to be acknowledged that in the appropriate measure God still "has provided the assistance of the Word for the sake of all those to whom he has been pleased to give useful instruction" (*Inst.* 1.6.3)?

That is to say, it seems to me that now there remains only one means of escape, which tends to be less and less appropriate, and that is to declare that a person's reprobation arises from the fact that one's neglect and one's resistance are stronger and more persistent than is divine grace. Otherwise, how does it come about that this is the fault of the human being and not God's? Is it not indeed always the case that a person's tyrannical desire is still a finite power, whereas the power of the divine Spirit through the Word is an infinite one? Moreover, must not those who want to assert the universality of Christ's redemption at any cost acknowledge this infinite power most of all? Further, must one not then say that in order truly to bring all people to blessedness, out of this infinite abundance God only had to multiply the summons addressed to every individual until such time as one's resistance should cease, thereby sufficiently demonstrating one's freedom to oneself and to the world, even if an absolute freedom—as just recently one famous Lutheran theologian[36] has admitted—is not compatible with the nature of any human creature? Suppose, moreover, that God does not increase the summons addressed to all persons in this way. At that point must one not say, in accordance with that doctrine of the decisive power of the final moment mentioned earlier, that God does not will to make all people truly blessed? It was precisely that infinite power of divine grace combined with God's creative omnipotence that ordered every concurrence and every event in the world that Augustine had in mind whenever he repeated such statements as this one:

> One should, therefore, have no doubt that human wills cannot resist the will of God who in heaven and on earth has done everything he willed . . . so that [the human] does not do what he wills, since [God] does what he wills and when he wills even with the very wills of human beings.[37]

Moreover, it was precisely this that Calvin also had in mind when he stated:

> For he is deemed omnipotent . . . because . . . he so regulates all things that nothing takes place without his deliberation . . . (and) upon whose nod depends whatever opposes our welfare. (*Inst.* 1.16.3)

Thus, if the situation with regard to this resistance is such that this resistance itself is conditioned by what God has ordered, and one can never refer to something that God has only foreseen and not already preordained,[38] then Dr. Bretschneider is quite right in saying that there is no other choice than that one can either accept the doctrine of divine grace together with the strict Augustinian doctrine of election,[39] or, as with Pelagius, abandon the doctrine of grace. Now, Dr. Bretschneider encourages his confessional partners to adopt the latter option on account of the intolerable and pernicious consequences further arising from the former strict doctrine of election. Moreover, in this he certainly does justice to Calvin and his followers since they themselves never drew these shocking consequences but always turned away from them. Precisely on this account, he nevertheless charges them, on their part, with logical inconsistency in view of the fact that they did not examine the relationship of these consequences to their propositions and that there could also remain no other choice for them than either to grant these conclusions as well or to abandon their statements on election and hence, together with these, the doctrine of divine grace as well.

This set of options clearly demonstrates the point on which the controversy has rested already for a long time now and it demonstrates how necessary it is to fight one's way through it once again if one is to struggle toward a meeting of minds in this matter. That is to say, this is how the matter has always stood, namely, that Calvin and his followers have always cast the reproach of Pelagianism at the opposing party, also *vice versa*, that their opponents have accused Calvin of those other conclusions, of which Dr. Bretschneider is also of a mind to disapprove. Lutheran theologians have attempted to parry this thrust and by means of artificial formulas to dismiss the accusations of Pelagianism, synergism, and semi-Pelagianism and also to base their repudiation of the Calvinian theory on the question of one's capacity to resist. Suppose that we consider Dr. Bretschneider to be the representative of this opinion. Then the matter would already have been settled from this side without any help from us. Yet, should there be certain persons who do not recognize him as such and who do not rightly know how to refute what has been said here by way of further clarification of his statements, they must nevertheless concede that, as long as one does not hide behind dim formulas but steps forth in the clear light of perception, the mere capacity to resist inevitably leads us back either to the Calvinian theory or over to a full-blown Pelagianism. This was exactly how matters stood on the other side, however. Calvin's followers always denied those conclusions that Calvin's opponents sought to impute to their doctrine. Yet, their opponents have never allowed these disavowals but have continually demanded of them either to concede these consequences or, if not, to modify in some way their doctrine of election itself. However, if they otherwise attribute any value to their conviction this is by no means a situation such that on account of it those who love truth and science can give up the struggle. Rather, suppose that there were error or pretense on one of the two sides. Every error has to be resolved by good will on both sides, and so too the artificially woven pretense of the person who claims the truth on one's own side will be exposed, unless one is not lacking in the necessary skills. Then both parties, in the conviction that they have the truth on their side, must engage in the struggle again and again in the hope that with more skill the controversy will be brought to a more favorable conclusion. Or, on the other hand, if the root of the controversy reaches down to the very depths of that way of thinking on which the original presuppositions are based and to which the controversy does not reach at that point, this fact must at least be clearly understood so that one knows that we cannot agree but that people so disposed will guard one meaning and vice versa those otherwise minded will guard the other meaning.

On this account we now wish to see whether we can come to as clear an understanding of what is to follow from the Calvinian theory as of what we have reached on the relationship of the Lutheran theory to the doctrine of human incapacity. However, I would like most of all to begin with the strict doctrine of election and its consequences for practical Christianity, for if we succeed in soothing the hearts and minds of people with regard to this matter both parties will be able to discuss more impartially the items that remain.

CALVIN ON ELECTION AND PRACTICAL CHRISTIANITY

Dr. Bretschneider, then, sums up (p. 99) these old complaints as follows: he distinguishes the person who already feels so far changed for the better as to count oneself among the elect, the person in whom virtue and vice are still at odds with each other and, finally, from the person who feels oneself to be incapable of breaking loose from the bonds of sin. He then summarizes the matter further in asserting that on the basis of the Calvinian theory the first person would be led to either folly or pride, the second to either folly or despondency, and the third to hopelessness. However, he continues, Calvin and those of his followers who did not get into this sorry mess simply had too strong a moral nature, too strong to have been able to find the otherwise natural application to life of this theoretical error. For my own part, from the start I have always been unable to believe that Calvin could have overlooked these consequences of his doctrine, since elsewhere he takes the defiance and despair of the human heart into such precise consideration as well as expressly saying how on this account one has to be very cautious and exact in presenting the doctrine. Accordingly, at the point at which he begins his discussion on the loss of the freedom of the will he puts the matter thus:

> The best way to avoid error will be to consider the perils that threaten man on both sides. (1) When man is denied all uprightness, he immediately takes occasion for complacency from that fact; and, because he is said to have no ability to pursue righteousness on his own, he holds all such pursuit to be of no consequence, as if it did not pertain to him at all. (2) Nothing, however slight, can be credited to man . . . without man himself falling into ruin through brazen confidence. (*Inst.* 2.2.1)

Thus, specifically with regard to the premise in connection with the doctrine of human incapacity arising at this point, was Calvin indeed supposed to have taken foolish pride and a disheartening sense of hopelessness into consideration and so to have taken stock of how one inevitably gives precedence to the one or the other as soon as one deviates even ever so slightly from the right course? Moreover, was he really supposed to have declared precisely this to be the proof,[40] as it were, of true and genuine doctrine in that it should do neither of these things? Then, in reaching the conclusion, namely, the doctrine of election itself, was he supposed to have forgotten this matter entirely and acted as though there were nothing further to be concerned about with regard to that twofold inclination of the human heart? It would be difficult for me to believe this of such a prudent teacher! Moreover, the fact that Calvin assigns the opposite meaning to the doctrine of human incapacity[41]—a meaning that ascribes not just a mere incapacity to human beings but openly adds all the terrible consequences of foolish pride—makes it indeed all the more unlikely that he should not raise the question as to what reproaches the opponents could bring against his own teaching, with regard to a disheartened sense of hopelessness least of all.

Therefore, it seems to me that the attempt would have to be made, nonetheless, to see if Calvin could not adduce something other than the admittedly rather weak proof of his own strict virtue, namely, something in the doctrine itself that could be cited in order to refute those inferences. It is certainly strange to me that I cannot refer directly to Calvin himself since in the place where he presents the doctrine of election, he says nothing more about how one must be on one's guard against assisting the constant inclination of the human heart always only to look for excuses. Yet, one should not conclude from this fact that since the two doctrines are so closely interconnected he had either stated the matter there once and for all, thus considering it here but not restating it, or that he did not deem it necessary to consider it here because there he believed that he had to address the beginning of the doctrine to everyone who, still finding themselves in their natural condition, should first be made disposed to accept the doctrine of divine grace. Here, however, after having set forth this doctrine, he now also assumes that there are readers who had allowed themselves to be led away from knowledge of the human incapacity to accept divine grace and thus in whom what divine grace effects had already operated.

Now, suppose Dr. Bretschneider presents Calvin with his example of such a person as this, who "has so far improved that one counts oneself among the elect," and that person says to Calvin, "Listen, surely you cannot object if, in turn, I also now allow a few sins to creep in, for God has elected me and improved my life. My blessedness is settled, and if I fall again, this certainly does not alter God's unchangeable decree, does it?" What will be Calvin's response to this person? Hardly any other answer than this: "I cannot know whether God has elected you. However, that it has not yet pleased God to change your life for the better—this I know for certain. This is so, for if you were truly changed and some sins had crept in against your will, you would of course console yourself with the thought that this could not alter the divine decree. Nevertheless, as one who is truly changed, how can you want to let sins creep in as well, for in fact the very beginning of a person's renewal, as you must already have learned from your Paul, consists in this, namely, that one does not willingly yield to sin[42] but keeps one's will pure—or if you prefer to use the language of your protector rather than mine and speak rather of virtue and vice and of good and evil rather than to speak as do my Paul and Augustine, also Luther and I, of belief and unbelief, and of flesh and spirit. Thus, if you take yourself to be a truly changed person and are, nonetheless, willing to allow sins to creep in, you deceive yourself with regard to one of those two things. The inconsistency is in yourself. Moreover, and you must not ascribe it to my teaching, for it is much rather the case that in this teaching you can find the standard that you seem to lack for testing yourself in this matter. That is to say, the person who is truly grasped in the process of sanctification and who devoutly trusts in one's election can never allow the desire to sin to arise in oneself, precisely because in the process of sanctification the Spirit of God bears witness that this person is a child of God.[43] Rather, it can arise in oneself only in unguarded circumstances. That is, it can arise in oneself in the absence of that devout trust,[44] but as soon as one recalls one's election and sanctification, or in short, one's state of grace, it must then become silent. Otherwise this state itself must be lost and that witness of the Spirit must fall silent. Thus, with regard to the unconscious and confused conditions of people, the doctrine can be arranged in no other way than that when carefully heeded it leads one back to the right consciousness and this is what my formulation of the doctrine will also do for you. However, in order to make you attentive to your confused discourse and to set a wholesome fear against the evil desire that drives you and thereby reestablish the equilibrium in which you are capable of receiving the truth, I will recall for you the words of Augustine, which, in my opinion, you all too often forget, namely, that those who have fallen afterward and who at that time seemed to us to live a pious life nevertheless did not really live, and although we did indeed consider them to be elect before God they were not and were not separated from the general mass of perdition.[45]

There is still no better mirror for you whatever than that entire treatise of this great teacher of the church. The reason is as follows. Just as the devout servant of God who is urged by the Spirit can do no other than admonish and correct those who stumble and those who are unrepentant, not knowing whether it will be of consequence for their salvation or their judgment,[46] so the person who would want to cease admonishing and correcting on account of being uncertain of the outcome would be merely a hireling.[47] Likewise, as he said, you can truly count on this: that if you have something of God's Spirit in you, this would also act against you in exactly the same way by not ceasing to admonish and correct you if you should want to let sin creep into the process as well. However, if you do not find this chastisement in yourself, then, according to my teaching, says Augustine, you will have no reason to believe that you are truly renewed; rather you must begin anew with my instruction and, convinced of your incapacity, learn above all to pursue the real love of the truth that does not deceive by lying and sincerely to desire the true freedom that does not long to return to the fleshpots of Egypt.[48] Then, he continues, if the doctrine of election still appears to you to be at all dangerous when your desire has been calmed by divine grace and you are a person who has truly changed for the better, we shall discuss it further.

Accordingly, in Calvin's understanding, the person who has been truly changed for the better is never led astray into folly on account of the doctrine of election, because such a person knows that one would then be deprived of the sign of election, for such a temptation can arise only for the reason that a person still lacks election,[49] and on that account Calvin then chides those who, with a somewhat tarnished but not undeserved reputation, accept such an excuse. However, just as little should one think of a wavering despair. Rather, according to Calvin's understanding of the matter, the person who has truly been renewed through faith effected by the divine Spirit holds to the Redeemer's Word: "Whoever believes in me has eternal life,"[50] and in having possession of eternal life one is so greatly assured that if a person's still remaining weaknesses are about to cause offense one always rediscovers the assurance of one's election in the ever reviving consciousness of one's faith made active in love. Hence, no one can really say that this activity is an "artificial bulwark,"[51] for it actually lies in the simple interconnectedness of the doctrine itself, and it is precisely this feature that is also to be found in the Solid Declaration.[52] However, with regard to the doctrine of election the rigorously consistent Calvin will have nothing whatsoever to do with the notion that one is truly renewed by means of one's own power, but rather, in Calvin's sense, through divine grace. And why indeed should he? For to be sure, for him, according to the heading that runs through the entire third book of the *Institutes* this doctrine is nothing other than that of the ways and means whereby the divine grace in Christ is to be received, whereas one who holds that notion has no wish to know anything of divine grace, hence for both of them there really still is no matter for controversy between the Solid Declaration and the *Institutes*.

Now, as far as the second person is concerned, in whom according to Dr. Bretschneider virtue and vice are still in conflict, Calvin has very little to say. In a favorable situation, such a person must think that one can indulge one's passions until the coming of grace, but in an unfavorable situation, that it would be to no purpose whatsoever to want to initiate any move toward change that, in any case, could never happen on account of one's already belonging to the former group. However, this much Calvin does say: first, that indeed not only in the unfavorable situation but also in the favorable one, a person would be quite right to think that it would be to no purpose to initiate anything toward truly changing one's life for the better. For one can initiate nothing whatsoever in this respect; only God can do this. Second, however, if one really sought to indulge one's passions, it would be wrong to say that virtue and vice were in contention for such a person. The reason for this is that holiness in life really occurs only in one's willing it. However, nothing at all makes gains toward holiness for the person who wills to indulge one's passions and produces a justification for doing it. In contrast, if a person were ever to strive after a pious life, that person should by no means think that one's efforts are in vain. This striving could never be the consequence of anything other than election itself[53] precisely because it is not this person who has initiated it but it is the divine Spirit instead.

Finally, to the third person, who feels incapable of improving one's life by oneself, Calvin would offer comfort and say to this person: if this wish for the improvement of which you speak is truly combined within yourself to this lively feeling of your incapacity and if you not only confess with your mouth but also have it in your heart,[54] then you should take care to guard yourself against the blasphemy of believing that God is hardening your heart. This is so, for this wish is certainly not a hardening but a softening, and you should accept it as a preliminary sign that you are already in touch with the divine Spirit, which alone is able to effect your renewal. Accordingly, for this person too, the doctrine of election will not prove to be a disadvantage to oneself or a cause for hopelessness. On the basis of all these cases, moreover, it would thus seem that it does not at all follow from the Calvinian doctrine of election, as Dr. Bretschneider claims on p. 98, that as consistently applied to life that doctrine could or would have to be very harmful to morality. On the contrary, it is only when views that are alien to that doctrine are compounded with it that it could perhaps become harmful. This possibility should, however, not be a reason to discredit the doctrine itself.

Yet, in accordance with what has been stated, it cannot be difficult to discover that in which the alien and compounded elements in the cases cited here are to be found. That is, it appears that Dr. Bretschneider presupposes the following: First he presupposes that someone could long for virtue or—to trade at least this more common and philosophical usage of speech, which I shall not say is pagan, for one that is theological—could long for the pious life, not in and of itself but only for the sake of blessedness as if blessedness were the end and the pious life were the means to that end, each being conceived as distinct from the other. He also presupposes that by means of such longing one could indeed have attained to a certain point in the holy life, as if by using this means one would be at a point assured of one's end, namely, blessedness, then would naturally want to return to one's passions and desires. This is not at all what Calvin's presupposes. From the very outset, Calvin told his followers that the holy life consists in the knowledge of God and that the knowledge of God lies in the knowledge of God's works and thus above all in knowledge of God's laws. Holding to Paul, Calvin also maintained that being awakened and born by the Spirit of God, the inner self delights in the law of God[55] and on account of this delight cannot wish to return to one's passions but always simply withdraws from them more and more. Thus, on the basis of Calvin's presupposition, a train of thought such as that conveyed above cannot stand at all, because the pious life and blessedness are one and the same thing, and when Calvin insisted that his doctrine of election should be diligently expounded to the people, he nonetheless certainly demanded only that it should only be presented in connection with his presuppositions. However, it seems to me that in that opposing presupposition of Dr. Bretschneider about longing for a holy life merely as a means to I know not what sort of entirely different blessedness no morality is anywhere to be found that could cause any harm to the doctrine of election. Yet, should Dr. Bretschneider want to grant that this is not actually a morality but that Calvin's doctrine does impede the very emergence of morality, I cannot agree with this point either, because the doctrine states precisely that the divine Spirit living and working in us never ceases to enlighten, to admonish, to rouse, and to pacify, and because, according to what that system claims, this is the only way in which morality can arise in the individual.

Further, no less strange is the fact that for all that Dr. Bretschneider has so wholly admitted that Calvin's doctrine of election is most intimately related to the doctrine of human incapacity, in that he wishes to demonstrate the right application of that doctrine to life, he then, nonetheless, introduces a person who wants to carry out the divine decree by oneself, without the divine Spirit and by one's own power, whereas according to Calvin its accomplishment depends upon faith active in love. Now, the fact that this claim has nothing to do with the matter and that such a person always rushes headlong toward one's ruin stands on every page Calvin wrote. Moreover, we have already had Calvin tell him this above (*Inst.* 2.2.1). Thus, he will not be at all surprised if already with their first steps our author's charges prove themselves to be divested of true understanding as well as of true virtue, and he will simply repeat that when it comes to understanding the divine mysteries anyone would be illumined only to the extent that one is enabled to be so by divine grace.[56] Indeed, perhaps he would maintain that persons holding any other opinion would also have to lose their way in folly or despair. This is so, for according to genuine Lutheran theory the doctrine of the forfeiture of grace[57] can just as well drive one person to folly or frighten another person into despair, depending on whether one thinks that on account of that forfeiture the safest thing is at all times to defer the state of grace until the inclinations and passions that would most readily lead one astray are finally stubbed out, or that the other person considers how easy it is to fall and also in this condition how easy it is to die and how all previous trouble and effort then will have been lost. Indeed, suppose that someone has a view to effect one's blessedness without grace and entirely on one's own, even if one has not gone so far as to attribute an infinite power to oneself. In considering how greatly one's own efforts could be either supported or impeded by circumstances and one's temptations could be either averted or heightened, depending on the nature of one's temperament, one can likewise fall into that rash despair that wants everything to depend on luck, or fall into that desolate despair that does indeed understand that everything lies in God's hands yet which still does not have the heart to trust God on account of the fact that blessedness can be granted to human beings only by grace.

However, although on p. 101 of the *Aphorisms* it is said to be dangerous to hold this view of blessedness, Calvin is far from considering his own doctrine of election to be endangered by it. On the contrary, he asks for nothing more than that the doctrine be grasped in terms of its proper interconnections and applied in its appropriate sphere. For him it is a scriptural doctrine, one that I myself consider to be such, and it is a misunderstanding for which I did not know that I had given occasion, when Dr. Bretschneider (*Aphorisms*, p. 102) seems to reproach me for wanting to sublimate it into an exercise for speculative philosophy. For myself, at least, the doctrines of the divine righteousness and the divine omnipotence[58] are also doctrines of the Christian church. However, as doctrines of scripture it is certainly Calvin's wish to have these doctrines presented only in the Christian church, in which scripture is believed, and he thus maintains that the Christian is to behold one's election only in Christ.[59] Given this stipulation, he promises not only a safe journey but also a pleasant one.[60]

Moreover, in the same passage Dr. Bretschneider cites (p. 101) the topic. There he seems, however, in part not to have pursued the topic far enough and also in part to have overlooked it. The topic refers to the fact that the danger inherent in a person's searching for blessedness is not so much to be found in one's doubt about election as much rather in the situation that the person is afflicted at the same time by a perverse desire to pursue a course in search of it outside the right one. This situation is precisely that of the person cited above, who rushes headlong into danger. However, doubts themselves should serve to prompt self-examination in the person who has not yet come to faith and to awaken that person, though for the person of faith they will disappear of themselves when one permits oneself to be guided by Calvin and when in the search for certainty about one's election one holds to those later signs which are the more sure testimonies of it.[61] "Then each person can know whether one lives in community with Christ,[62] and in this one has a sufficiently clear testimony that one's name is written in the book of life."[63] "This efficacious calling"[64] ... "is the first evidence of election and justification is the second."[65] "Moreover, the person who has once come under the protection of Christ in this way is also certain that just as he did for Peter, Christ petitions and requests on one's behalf that one's faith will indeed not cease."[66]

However, if Calvin admits that doubts about one's election can also arise for the believer too and that this makes such an instruction necessary, he does not seek the reason for this in the fact that election is dependent solely upon God's will and that persons are incapable of achieving their salvation by themselves. Rather he seeks the reason for this based on the question of the whence of the revelation of their salvation, for in this respect every person would like to have it in a more evident form in a higher degree of Christian perfection or in a more manifest way in communicable letters.[67] This is the reason Calvin's cure for this doubt is to be found solely in his drawing one's attention to the ongoing work of the Holy Spirit in the soul of the person of faith. Thus, if one will only agree with Calvin that it is the Holy Spirit alone who makes the divine decree effective in the elect, and if with him one acknowledges that there is no practical Christianity other than that of the free governance of this Spirit, one then sees no disadvantage to a practical Christianity arising from a doctrine that is nothing other than the simple expression of the natural feeling evoked by the activity of this Spirit, which dwells wherever it will.[68] However, if, on the one hand, one indeed wants to acknowledge how closely Calvin's doctrine is related to that of human incapacity and that of divine grace, yet, on the other hand, wants nonetheless to apply this doctrine to a praxis that is not dependent on divine grace and is supposed to arise from human self-sufficiency—a praxis, however, that Calvin would perhaps not at all have called even properly Christian—then disadvantages for such a practical Christianity would certainly have to arise. Yet, Calvin and his followers remain safe from these disadvantages and nothing other follows from this consideration than that one should not mix two different doctrines together, for they will only undermine each other.

Given this clarification, it is to be hoped that we have now cleared away from the Calvinian doctrine the notion that if it is strictly followed it would destroy one's striving after sanctification. Its Pelagian opponents[69] will have convinced themselves that Augustinian Christians also have a practical Christianity and that in this matter they are not in the least troubled on account of their doctrine of predestination. Those opponents of the Calvinian doctrine who in principle are themselves Augustinian[70]—though without here demanding from them a decision as to whether they or the Calvinists are the more consistent—nevertheless have to grant that the Spirit of God is just as active to effect in them their own sanctification and that of others without feeling that this admission is dependent upon their view of the doctrine of election.

ELECTION AND THE HUMAN FACULTIES

Now, having disposed of these matters it is my hope that those still outstanding may be considered more calmly by both parties. May this be so, for it is certainly difficult to dispute with a person in requisite calm and with a view to a favorable outcome when one harbors the opinion that one's interlocutor is taking a path on which one cannot travel farther without at the same time renouncing both virtue and happiness and surrendering to despair and vice. It is then that the love that is disquieted all too easily hampers the precision that controversy demands, and because one wishes just as much to affect as to convince one also multiplies the less cogent reasons with the result that the opponent who is not moved by the same interests withdraws oneself all the more easily from the trap. It seems to me, then, that in the past, and also even more recently, this has always been the way that things have fared in the controversy surrounding the doctrines of Augustine and Calvin. This being so, we shall undertake a little sorting out to determine those objections that are still valid and those that are not in accordance with the acknowledged premise.

For example, in this connection it is stated in the *Aphorisms* (p.102), "On that rock on which it is so difficult not to founder if one accepts the doctrine of predestination one will inevitably be driven upwards by the striving that necessarily arises from reason to search for the highest precepts of divine wisdom." However, once it is granted that the Augustinian doctrine of election strictly follows from the doctrine of human incapacity, then precisely from this doctrine it follows that human reason has to be prevented from seeking to penetrate the depths of the divine wisdom, because on account of its incapacity reason would necessarily have to become confused. Still, reason that is persuaded of its incapacity and illumined by the divine Spirit also wants to get to know the divine wisdom, but reason seeks it only from scripture and from one's own experience and has no wish to go beyond this. The former activity is the subject of all that Calvin preaches; the latter activity is all that he warns against.

Hence, on this matter the symbolic writings of the Lutheran church, which proceed on the same presupposition of human incapacity, also contain exactly the same teaching.[71]

Similarly, among the other demonstrable doctrines belonging to the system and to scripture with which Calvin's theory is in conflict, Dr. Bretschneider (p. 96) also includes belief in the moral freedom of persons, in that the theory asserts that all persons had lost the capacity to fulfill the moral law. However, the system of the Lutheran church does indeed affirm this loss just as decidedly and openly as does the Calvinian theory. In fact, this statement is simply another expression of that doctrine of human incapacity and already in itself it is clear that if one statement in a system asserts the human incapacity for what is good then it is impossible that another statement in the same system could assert such a moral freedom of persons that it would include the capacity to fulfill the will of God. It is much rather the case that according to the system of the Lutheran church as well, this freedom first begins with the situation of the person who has been forgiven and reborn, which is precisely a birth into this freedom. However, to the natural person the system allows freedom only in relation to worldly things, a freedom that enables one to overcome one's desires by means of insight[72] and to conquer the impulse toward self-sufficiency through the impulse toward sociality.[73] Still, neither that insight nor this impulse is of itself capable of fulfilling the divine law. Nevertheless, Dr. Bretschneider subsequently (p. 103) withdraws this reproach to a certain extent, in that he grants that the doctrine of election does not really have to do with the question of the relationship of moral freedom to God's rule[74] even though previously he has asserted that God's rule dissolves[75] the moral nature in order to exalt God's free choice.[76]

For this reason, we shall no longer continue to dwell on this matter for the moment; nor shall we pursue further another matter, even though it is one that frequently arises (p. 42 and p. 98), namely, that this doctrine is in conflict with repeated and earnest exhortations that the sinner should improve oneself and seek after one's salvation, for this has already been answered in passing above with reference to Augustine's little book *On Rebuke and Grace*. Or, in the same way as we declare ourselves to be persons who ourselves admonish and correct others, must we not also declare that the holy men of God[77] in scripture as well as those outside it have been urged on by the same Spirit to do exactly this? Moreover, is it not obvious that it is only by means of challenges by the Spirit that the sinner can actually come to an immediate consciousness either of one's incapacity or of one's obduracy? That is to say, suppose that a person observes that one's capacity to act is rendered inactive by one's own supposed[78] willing. Then the person would have to feel, nonetheless, that a human being cannot take oneself to be able to do anything, other than what the Spirit can, which awakens and stimulates the slumbering will.

ELECTION AND THE BREADTH OF BLESSEDNESS

Thus, we shall leave this matter and move on quickly to that main objection, which above all caused Luther and Melanchthon to deviate from Augustine's strict doctrine and which is also still considered valid by all those who, like Calvin, proceed on the basis of the presupposition of human incapacity, namely, that the strict doctrine of predestination is in conflict with the scriptural doctrine of universal redemption through Christ. In the *Aphorisms* this objection is presented in three different forms.

First (p. 96), the Calvinian theory is said to claim that the measures taken by God to restore moral freedom are intended only for some and not for all. Second (p. 98), his theory is said to be in conflict with the solemn affirmation of the Apostle (Rom. 5:12–19) that redemption through Christ is just as universal and extended to all human beings as sin and its punishments are universal. Then, finally (p. 103), the entire doctrine is said to have to do with the statement as to whether it is God's will that the entire human race, which is deserving of damnation on account of original sin, will be saved through Christ and whether God denies the means to that end to no one, or whether this is not what God wills and that therefore God withholds the means to that end from some. Certainly, it is not to no purpose that the learned author has presented this objection in three different places and forms, hence it is our responsibility to try to derive our own view from each of these statements and to grant it our own treatment.

First, then, regarding the statement that the Calvinian theory asserts the measures God adopts to restore moral freedom are intended only for some and not for all: now, in order to avoid any mistakes we shall immediately change this plural to a singular, for the church knows only the one measure taken by God for the restoration of human beings, namely, through Jesus Christ.

Now, the fact that not all persons will actually be restored through Christ but that some are pardoned and others lost is as much accepted by the Lutheran church as by Calvin. All that matters, on that account, is how God intended[79] the measure God took. Now, the Lutheran church states that God has intended redemption for all but that those who did not accept it became lost on account of their resistance. So, does this mean contrary to the divine intention? It is certainly difficult to assert this, however, for once it is accepted that this is God's intention, God must also intend rightly. Thus, one has to assert that God has intended redemption in such a way that everyone could be redeemed but that also those who would not wish to accept it would be lost. We shall see later on that Calvin can also agree with this point, yet that this is simply a point at which he cannot stop but is rather of the opinion that God must have ordained things in such a way that some must resist. Now, if we simply disregard the constantly perplexing notion of a particular divine decree with reference to the individual person and hold only to the incontestable way in which God has ordained that the gospel should be spread abroad and also to the way in which God has preordained how human matters were to have taken shape, then we would have to say that on the basis of both of these convictions taken together it necessarily follows from the divine decree that not everyone whom the gospel reached could accept it. Precisely because the gospel arose from within a historical context and was spread abroad by means of human language and influence, it could also take no other course than that of history in general, with the result that only some few out of a great stirring among people would actually be formed and gathered to the new life, and only as this ceaseless expansion and contraction were repeated would the new and living whole gradually increase.

Judaism could not have endured without zealots who held the rest of the people together, yet among those who are zealous for that which was yet to be fulfilled there would also have to be false ones, who in order to cling to former things would also have to spurn those things that are new and better. Had there not been such persons, Judaism would have disintegrated long ago, and only by means of the same would it have been possible for Christianity to have been nourished and protected in its fragile beginnings. If this were the case, there must also have been those who rejected Christianity. In contrast, it is the same with respect to the Gentiles, among whom there would be a formidable mass of corruption. When some were to have attached themselves to a people like the Jews, who were otherwise so scorned, Christianity passed over to the Gentiles. However, among that mass there also had to have been those who scorned Christianity. Thus, here it seems that a successful outcome on the one hand, not different from a failed one on the other, was intended at the same time, for it is inconceivable that something would gradually expand without any resistance, and there can be no resistance that does not include some who remain under its constraint until death.

I wish to put this forward only as a preliminary suggestion, not as a strict argument. However, the expression "to intend" does also invite one to drop such a hint; and from what has been stated I draw no other conclusion than that if we look at the matter under the aspect of "intending," this observation conforms more to the Calvinian formula, which views God as being equally active in preordaining[80] with regard both to those who will be pardoned and those who will be lost. This is so, in that the one follows from the divine power of the gospel and the other from its human character, but it is not in accordance with that formula which assumes that God's foreordaining applies only to the one but not to the other,[81] precisely because the attainment of the one to salvation cannot be intended without also intending the departure from salvation of the other. Moreover, this is precisely how Paul[82] presents his assessment of the matter. That is to say, as Paul observed one period of time elapse after another without any acceptance of the gospel by the people of Israel as a whole he could not conceal the fact that *proslēpsis*[83] (Rom. 11:15) does not apply to the same individuals as does *apobolē*.[84] Rather, when he showed the condition[85] of both to be the same, he meant the people in the succession of its generations, whereas the lost would remain lost and only out of their *paraptōma*[86] could there come the *sōtēria*[87] of the Gentiles.

Now, second, to this point there is nevertheless set in contrast[88] another solemn assurance from the same Apostle, namely, that redemption through Christ is just as universal and extended to all human beings as sin and its punishments are universal; however, as Dr. Bretschneider asserts, the Calvinian theory is in conflict with this assurance. Yet, before entering into a discussion of this matter, I cannot withhold a general comment regarding the way in which use is generally made of scriptural passages in these and in other dogmatic controversies, for I also find that Dr. Bretschneider does the same in this regard. On pages 87–94 he holds that the Lutheran theory is based on explicit and clear passages of scripture, whereas the Calvinian theory only makes inferences and deductions with which those explicit and clear passages are in conflict.

Now, I think that this is a distinction, which is certainly important for the popular use of scripture precisely because, on the one hand, not all of the inferences and deductions can follow, whereas, on the other hand, that which is explicit and clear makes a better impression on people. However, in my opinion when it comes to the scholarly study of scripture this is a matter that he should by no means have introduced. The reason for this is that each passage is clear only in relation to[89] its context. Further, that which is literal can also be taken to be explicit only to the extent that the context has determined how literally it must or must not be understood. Hence, all inferences and deductions as well are nothing other than determinations shaped by the context, so that between the two there is basically no difference whatsoever. The most serious aspect of the matter, however, is that once one has accepted the distinction it is scarcely possible even for the most impartial and unbiased person to apply it objectively and fairly.[90] Instead one's dogmatic views then exert an influence on one's hermeneutical investigations.

For example, Dr. Bretschneider considers 1 Tim. 2:4 to be an explicit and clear passage in support of the Lutheran theory. There, of course, it is stated that God desires all persons "to be saved and to come to the knowledge of the truth." However, since the sole aim of the passage is simply to demonstrate that intercession is well-pleasing to God, and since *pantōn anthrōpōn*[91] in v.1 is used in a very loose way in that *basileis*[92] and *en huperoxē ontes*[93] can simply be removed without in any way further dividing the whole, one has to be very doubtful whether one can treat it in an any more exact sense than the expression *pantas anthrōpous*.[94] Thus, I would rather deny that one can do so and hardly take this passage to be an explicit and clear proof-text, because after all it is only incidental and is to be traced back to a statement[95] that is taken to be imprecise. Further, just how does the matter stand with regard to Titus 2:11, where, of course, the reference is to "all persons" though in no respect with regard to their destiny but rather with regard to "an appearing" for all? Now, Paul certainly could not literally say that at that time grace in Christ had already appeared to all persons, hence one sees all the more clearly how little one should in general take an expression such as "all persons" literally unless a yet more specific emphasis is placed on it. There, however, it is only stated that the saving grace that has appeared to all persons is a grace that "trains" us, we Christians, in a pious and disciplined life in the world, therefore in no respect does the passage prove anything of a specific nature against the Calvinian doctrine. Indeed, to this doctrine itself, this distinction between "all persons" to whom grace has appeared, and "us," we Christians whom it actually trains, can quite easily apply with equal validity. Moreover, if I may speak directly to the matter, the other passages are even weaker still, for even Jesus' command to go "into all the world"[96] can prove nothing further than that in part the attempt should be made to reach all persons so that they would be "without excuse,"[97]— which indeed Calvin and Augustine also frequently cited as the purpose of the universal proclamation address to all—and in part that from among all nations some should be blessed[98] through Christianity. However, in order for this to happen it must be proclaimed universally among all nations, and this certainly is demonstrated over against Jewish particularism though not over against any Calvinian one.

On the other hand, when Dr. Bretschneider attempts to dismiss the Calvinian proof-texts he himself infers distinctions from them, which not only are not present in the text, but which are also directly contrary to the entire way of thinking of the New Testament. For example, he notes that it is only a worldly privilege that some from among so many first became Christians and teachers of Christianity and that this has nothing to do with blessedness in the world to come. This certainly would be so if these were the divinely chosen ones only as those who became Christians earlier, the others only later. However, in contrast to these one must also necessarily set those who were also included within the compass of proclamation but who did not become Christians at all. Moreover, when Dr. Bretschneider offers the opinion that it is nonetheless nowhere stated that God did not also will to save those who did not become Christians, a view that is so decidedly contrary to the New Testament way of thinking that it is not worth citing any specific passages on the matter to show that those who disrespect the proffered grace are lost, that salvation depends upon faith in Christ, and that only those who believe in Christ will also be where he is.[99]

The case is the same with the following distinction, namely, that in all of these passages it is a question of a choice among Jews and Gentiles and not of a choice among Christians. To be sure, the fact that persons do or do not become Christians is simply a matter of it being in accordance with the divine ordering. Still, do not people today become Christians over time? Will all become Christians or only some and not others? Thus, is not the issue here, as well as that recognized in the symbolic books of both churches precisely the same complaint: that among many who are called only few are chosen,[100] but here also stated in relationship to an order and choice according to which persons become Christians? This is so, for whether a person born within Christendom experiences the activities of preparatory grace alone or also those of efficacious grace, the divine ordering must have played precisely as much a part in this process as when a Jew or a Gentile becomes a person of faith and is baptized, or is only called. Nor is the situation any better in those passages which Mr. Bretschneider cites as being expressly opposed to the Calvinian theory, namely, those in which the ground of rejection is said to be an unwillingness to draw near and an unwillingness to accept. That is to say, when indeed had Augustine and Calvin ever denied this?

It is still the case that both parties share these passages in common, and only at this point does the question arise concerning the nature of the relationship of the divine ordering and foreseeing to this unwillingness. Only at this point, moreover, does Augustine respond and then along with him Calvin:

> God, nonetheless, did this only through the wills of human beings, since he undoubtedly had omnipotent power over human hearts to turn them to where he pleased.[101]

The case is also precisely the same with regard to the solemn assurance of the Apostle in Rom. 5:12–19 with which the Calvinian theory is said to be in conflict. In any case, one cannot explicitly and clearly cite this biblical passage, which is made multiply complex by its problematic structure, and overall it is certainly not possible to argue from it in such a careless manner. However, with regard to this solemn assurance "that redemption through Christ is just as universal and equally extended to all human beings as sin and its punishments are universal"[102] one has to ask whether it is at all possible that Paul really granted this? That is to say, since, he asserts that all persons actually sin and actually die, he would also have to assert that all persons would actually be redeemed and actually be saved. However, just as he does not assert this elsewhere, neither does he offer this assurance here but expressly states ". . . *hoi tēn perisseian tēs xaritos . . . lambanonvtes en zōē basileusousin . . .*"[103] and one clearly also has to explain *eis pantas anthrōpous* (v.18)[104] accordingly. Thus at best, one can say that with this increasingly emphatic repetition Paul's intention is to state that if not everyone is to be saved through Christ just as through Adam they all died, the reason for this is not the redeeming power that is to be found in Christ, viewed in and of itself. However, precisely this can also be said without invalidating Calvin's theory. This is so, for as Calvin says of the first Adam in *Inst.* 1.15.8: "In this integrity man by free will had power, if he so willed, to attain eternal life. Here it would be out of place to raise the question of God's secret predestination because our present subject is not what can happen or not, but what man's nature was like." Thus, of the other Adam, Calvin could also say that if the question does not concern what will or can happen or not but concerns instead what power lay in him, then here the question of predestination has been quite prematurely intermixed. Instead we simply have to grant that according to its inner power redemption was universal. This means that even if the number of persons of faith was to increase ever so much, the power of redemption to make all persons righteous and to make them blessed would never be exhausted. We would also have to admit that as long as the Word went forth to a person and the Holy Spirit effected in this person the beginning of faith, one's forgiveness could therefore never be left outstanding. Redemption, otherwise, would perchance not have been destined for that person, if too little room had been afforded that person to receive redemption.

Having now had the opportunity to demonstrate the second way in which the *Aphorisms* present the same objection and having shown how easy it is to be mistaken and misled in one's assessment of scriptural proofs, we now finally come to the third way. On p. 103 Dr. Bretschneider expressly claims the following: the entire doctrine has to do with the question of whether God wills that the entire human race which is deserving of damnation on account of original sin will be saved through Christ and whether God denies the means to that end to none, or whether this is not what God wills and that therefore God withholds the means to that end from some. However, to this way of presenting the issue I would like to raise two objections. For one thing, the Lutheran church certainly does not assert that in every way and in every sense God wills that all persons will be saved through Christ. The reason given is that there is indeed a will of God that is omnipotent; yet, if with this omnipotent will God had willed that all persons should be saved everyone would also actually have to be saved and those who could not be saved God should not have created at all in the first place. Now, in contrast, there is of course that part of the Lutheran church which also begins from the assumption of human incapacity and of the need for faith which has to be effected by the Holy Spirit through the Word. This part of the church even admits that only a few persons receive the Word of God in earnest and sincerely obey it[105] and that many from among those who once accepted it joyfully afterwards fall away from it in turn. Thus, either it must be granted that in accordance with that omnipotent will, God did not will the salvation of those who fall away and of those who do not accept it but that God willed this simply in accordance with some other will, or the omnipotent will of God must be wholly denied or at least denied within the sphere of human freedom. This would be opposed to the warning of a distinguished Lutheran theologian who, although his statements are not always easy to unravel, at least has this to say about the matter, namely, that "the recollection of the doctrine of election can still be salutary as setting limits to the presumptions of moral philosophy when it postulates an absolute freedom of human beings that is incompatible with the nature of a creature."[106] Or would this limit not also be the demand of an absolute freedom if this freedom were not included in the activity of the divine omnipotence such that through this human freedom nothing could occur that had not been ordained by that divine freedom? However, even if one were to seek to limit the divine omnipotence by means of human freedom and say that those who fall away or those who do not accept grace are not saved and that one must stand by the fact that the final reason for this is their own will, what should one say with regard to those to whom the Word does not reach at all? Of these persons the confessional writings of the Lutheran church themselves express the matter as follows: "To many peoples and nations God does not grant God's Word or takes it away from them,"[107] and they do not attempt to shift responsibility for the matter from God's will but rather exactly like Calvin, explain it wholly by the fact that God owes us nothing[108] and that it is to be presented as an act of God's righteousness—which latter point I leave open for the moment and will consider hereafter.

Thus, on this basis that portion of the Lutheran church itself acknowledges that the will of God is that they should not be made blessed through the Word—for "not granting" and "taking away" is certainly very much a matter of the will—and that God denies them the means thereto. However, should one be able to say that one portion of the Lutheran church has abandoned the doctrine of human incapacity and is of the opinion that "it is nowhere stated that God does not indeed also want to make blessed those who are not Christians" (*Aphor.* p. 92), this group could certainly help themselves out and say: God indeed does not will that they should become Christians through the Word, yet God does will that they become Christians without the Word in that they achieve their blessedness by themselves. Still, what great help is this if one of them (*Aphor.* p. 102, footnote)—someone who does not want to be prevented from searching out the depths of the divine wisdom since reason inevitably reaches out toward it in its function of searching out the highest principles of wisdom, refusing both the Calvinian and the Lutheran veto[109] of reason as in no respect either natural or appropriate—if such a person inquires further and asks, "Will everyone then actually save themselves?" and after this question has been answered in the negative goes on to ask, "Why not? Could their reason not possibly be assisted by external circumstances and made more effective? Or is it a weak will that they have already received from God? Moreover, apart from one's will, what else has a person received from God whereby one can strengthen a will that is weak?" What, indeed, is to be done about this person? Either one would trace the matter back to the omnipotent will of God who created one person to have become like this at the end of one's life and created another person like that, or one would trace it back to a wholly groundless will in the human being, a will which entirely obviates divine sovereignty in human matters so that nothing remains to it other than to have willed and created this groundless will.

These remarks are only incidental, nevertheless, for the presupposition that a person's self-sufficiency enables one to achieve one's blessedness does not constitute the basis for the controversy being carried on between the two churches, nor on the basis of this assumption can one inquire about a will of God to make all persons blessed through Christ. Moreover, as far as I am concerned, I have been strongly critical with regard to this matter not in order to sublimate the controversy into being an exercise for speculative philosophy but rather simply to offer a thorough account of the cases presented to us in such a way that we will arrive at the boundaries of the purely theological domain.

Now, at this point it seems to me that the matter stands as follows: there is one universal characteristic of redemption, which the Calvinian doctrine expounds just as well as does the Lutheran doctrine, namely, that as concerns the indwelling power of the act of redemption through Christ—and here one looks at the sacrifice of Jesus or at the teaching of Jesus or at the means of grace, which he instituted—nothing stands in the way of any person's being made holy and blessed through Christ as long as God guides matters in such a way that the Word reaches a person that the Holy Spirit can unite that person with Christ through faith.[110] In *Inst.* 3.1.1 Calvin himself expresses this sufficiently clearly, and I simply draw attention to the following words: ". . . as long as Christ remains outside us, and we are separated from him, all that he has suffered and done for the salvation of the human race remains useless and is of no value to us."

Then, "Christ so 'came by water and blood' (1 John 5:6–7), lest the salvation imparted through him escape us." Augustine also states, "And who loved the weak more than he who became weak for all and was crucified for all because of this weakness?"[111]

However, there is also another universal characteristic of redemption which the Lutheran church—inasmuch as it still acknowledges that faith has to be effected through the Holy Spirit—tolerates just as little as does the Calvinian, namely, the universality of the outcome that all persons would actually come to be justified and blessed through Christ.[112] The two churches really differ, moreover, only in the way in which the opposite of this universal characteristic is to be expressed, in that the one church says that some will not be saved because God did not will to grant them faith whereas the other church says that some will not be saved because God foresaw that they would not accept faith, which with regard to the universality of redemption clearly makes no difference whatever.[113] Thus, if the followers of Calvin have allowed themselves to be driven to make negative statements here, statements they were not forced to make by the actual nature of their teaching, this has to be attributed not to the doctrine but to its clumsy defense. In contrast, those who are of the opinion that persons must generate faith from within themselves do indeed to some extent come close to those who assert that persons really can aid themselves in ways other than through faith. Yet, the latter also want only to set the universality of blessedness in the place of the universality of redemption, and at that point they too uphold a two-fold universality just as much, such that one person must be accepted but another denied. This is the case, in that what they are saying is this: in the reason attributed to the human race, viewed in itself, there is sufficient power to lead everyone to perfection and by means of it to blessedness, but life does not develop reason in every individual to this same degree. Consequently, no distinction whatsoever appears here unless one assumes that all persons are made completely equal. However, if we keep to the assumption of the ancient church, we have to say that in this matter the two churches are in agreement that rightly understood the Word of Christ is a universal Word whereas the work of the Holy Spirit is a particular work.

QUESTIONS CONCERNING THE SO-CALLED TWOFOLD WILL OF GOD

Now, we have no need to be apprehensive about what seem to be the disadvantageous consequences either for practical Christianity or for the general theory of Christianity that have been attributed to the Calvinian theory by its opponents. Neither can we be at all inclined either to abandon its presupposition, on account of consequences that are said to follow from the conclusion drawn, or instead of this strict conclusion to fall back on one that is less rigorous, whereby the presupposition itself would again be partially annulled. However, here we must of necessity ask ourselves, "What was it that moved the Lutheran church, which of course also proceeded on the basis of Augustine's teachings, to abandon this particular point, and how did it conceal from itself the fact that with its formulation of the doctrine of election it certainly did obscure the mutually shared presupposition of the indispensability of divine grace?" Now, one can hardly answer that question in any other way than this: "It shrank from the rigor and strictness of the statement that God definitely should not will both that some persons would be blessed and that the divine predestination should be the ultimate reason that some would be condemned." Moreover, in order to avoid this quandary, what is assumed, on the one hand, is a twofold will of God which was indeed also presented in the patristic and scholastic treatments of the matter, namely, one will of God that was—to express it in the more recent language of the *Aphorisms*—proposed "with a view to the idea"[114] of the blessing[115] of all fallen human beings, and another will by virtue of the fact that "in experience" not all persons will, nonetheless, "actually be made blessed," or—in terms of the longer established way of putting it—a prevenient will and a subsequent will of God. However, on the other hand, if I may put it this way, it also assumed a half will of God, in that it states that predestination extends only to the elect and not at all to the reprobate, also that these persons will be condemned apart from any such divine will as that through which the elect will come to be blessed. Now, as far as the first distinction is concerned, it is the same as that which dogmatic theologians sought to express with the terms prevenient and subsequent will, and it is also generally accepted that those who are in agreement with the Calvinian formula do not assume such a distinction. Hence, it is not altogether correct when Dr. Bretschneider (p. 85) states that, according to the Calvinian doctrine, the will of God even in its idea intended only a certain number of persons to be made blessed. This is not correct, for of anyone who does not at all assume such a contrast between willing as idea and as realization or between prevenient and subsequent willing, it cannot also be said that in this person's opinion something would happen both in accordance with the one will and in accordance with the other will. Rather, on this understanding, Calvin's opinion is already misrepresented in that it does not simply reject some particular use of this distinction out of hand, but has no need of the distinction at all. One must rather say that Calvin's doctrine is based on the fact that he was quite unable to imagine such distinctions with regard to the will of God. Moreover, strictly speaking, this applies not only to this distinction but to any similar one, and Calvin's defenders, even if some also seem to use such a distinction, either abandon it or condescend to their opponents by speaking with them in their own language but indeed without sharing their opinion, a move which is always questionable in that it gives rise to fresh misunderstandings. Now, it is primarily and precisely for this reason that I could never have done otherwise than also to adhere to the Calvinian formula, because I cannot understand such distinctions.

The terms "prevenient" and "subsequent" imply a distinction in time, and this is also a matter that has been discussed frequently enough. Now, to be sure, those who defend this distinction state that in no respect does it involve any change in the divine will, taking one direction prior to a given event and taking a different direction thereafter. However, already based on the different explanations that they offer, one sees that the division of will is made only for the sake of the particular case that is the subject of discussion here. That is to say, some[116] trace the distinction to the divine attributes and state that the prevenient will, namely, that all persons should be blessed, is the will of the divine mercy, whereas the subsequent will, namely, that persons not of faith will be condemned, is the will of the divine justice. Now, I will not even discuss the point that God cannot have one attribute with a will that is different from that of another attribute. If this were so, it would destroy the oneness of God's being. Rather, I will simply recall the fact that the will by means of which persons of faith then definitively come to be actually blessed must indeed be the same will as that by means of which persons not of faith actually come to be condemned. This accords with the more recent explanation from Bretschneider when it states that in God's idea God intends blessedness for all humans beings, but in the realization of blessedness God grants it only to some. It must be the same will, for it is quite easy to reply here that by means of the intending will even the elect are not actually made blessed but rather by means of the granting will. Moreover, either no will whatsoever to predestine the individual can lie in the intending will and it is therefore completely non-efficacious and void, or blessedness has to lie in a two-sided will.

According to the earlier way of explaining it the matter is not so simple, for the fact that persons of faith come to be blessed is not ascribed to the divine justice but precisely to the divine mercy. However, from this consideration, it follows only that one would have to differentiate and ascribe a twofold will to the divine mercy, a universal but non-efficacious will that all persons are to be blessed and a particular will in accordance with which persons of faith actually do come to be blessed.[117] Alternately there could also be some who would not exactly care to commend even Augustine in all respects and who would wish to dispute this and argue that persons of faith would not come to be blessed by means of the divine justice because they really had earned a right thereto through the divine promise and because justice involves abiding by one's word. Moreover, even if one would not want to concede this point, one would still have to grant that in general terms to distinguish persons of faith from persons not of faith is proper to divine justice because all justice is based on making distinctions, whereas mercy makes none. Thus, once again, the prevenient will makes no distinctions but is completely non-efficacious, whereas the efficacious will of God is the subsequent will, which does make distinctions. More-over, if it is then supposed that the prevenient and subsequent will of God are nevertheless not to signify any change or any distinction in time, then the efficacious divine will that does make distinctions is from both points of view the same and also eternally the same as the non-efficacious will. Yet, how God can have an efficacious will and a non-efficacious will with regard to the same matter is precisely something that I, like Calvin, cannot understand.

In response to this it will of course be said that this distinction between an efficacious and non-efficacious will of God must nevertheless be con-ceded in every case in relation to the divine laws, because these laws are not fulfilled. However, I do commend Calvin for not wanting to inter-mix these two concepts of "divine command" and "divine will"[118] chiefly because evil persons, in that they commit an evil deed, still do accomplish that which God willed should happen even though thereby they certainly act against God's command, and also because even good persons are always able only to fulfill the divine commands in an approximate way. However, if we would want to say that God's will is done only imperfectly, then we would have to abjure[119] divine omnipotence. Yet, if the divine command is divided in this way, then that distinction of wills is shown to be completely null and void, and in accordance with this explanation the prevenient will of God is precisely for this reason no will of God, because it would be a non-efficacious one. Conversely, had someone understood the statement "that all people should be blessed" as a command of God to mean that all people are to act in such a way that everything is up to them if they are all to become blessed, this view would conflict very little with the Calvinian doctrine. Rather, Augustine and Calvin themselves have stated it often enough.[120]

The other way around, others explain the prevenient and subsequent will of God in this way: that the object of the former is the human being as human being, whereas that of the latter is the condemned as the con-demned. Now, here I infer the same features as before, namely, that the believer as well comes to be blessed not as a human being but as a per-son of faith. Consequently, on both sides the efficacious will of God is the same will of God, or namely, the subsequent will of God, whereas the pre-venient will is non-efficacious, because nothing happens to a human being simply as a human being. The distinction is simply this: this explanation avoids tracing the twofold will to the divine attributes precisely because it is felt to be so difficult to do this and because the preference is to relate the will of God to the contrast between the universal and the particular. However, if this is the more correct move and one can say of God that for God the universal and the particular are different objects, are they then to be understood as objects of cognition or of willing? That is to say, it is indeed only because of the imperfection of our knowledge that for us the oneness of what is universal is different from the totality of what is particular and our knowledge is so much the more genuine and lively the more the two merge together. It is only when we can develop the range, quantity, and diversity of individual things belonging to one genus from the concept of interconnectedness with the whole genus, as known, only then does the universal concept emerge out of the abstract and lifeless calculated total to become a living intuition.[121] Thus, how much more must we rather say that in the divine knowledge the two merge together? So, then we must say that in the divine knowledge what is universal and what is particular must be completely merged, and that if we imagine that in God as well the one is separated from the other, an anthropomorphism creeps up on us and indeed one that is not unavoidable.

Now, when it is a matter of willing, the situation is precisely the same. The reason for this is that it is also certainly on account of our deficiency that we predict something in general terms, which is to say merely according to its possibility. Thereafter, however, when individual cases occur in their distinctness, the will becomes divided. However, one cannot think of such a general and unspecific will in God, because one must think only of the most distinct knowledge of the objects of God's will and not of a will that is indistinct. If God condemns the condemned simply as condemned then God also forgives[122] the person of faith simply as a person of faith. Apart from both of these decisions, however, I do not know how to express any divine will with regard to the blessedness of human beings as human beings other than always precisely as follows: namely, that from among human beings persons of faith are forgiven[123] for the sake of Christ, whereas because they are outside of Christ persons not of faith are condemned. So, I would also be glad to moderate these statements, but I cannot wish to do this at such a price that I ascribe to God a twofold will with regard to the same object and thereby destroy the oneness of God's being.

Moreover, the situation is precisely the same with regard to that half will, namely, that God's predestination applies only to the elect whereas with regard to the condemned God has not foreseen or ordained anything but has only foreknown what will befall them. This is the case, for if God's foreknowing extends beyond God's foreordaining, God's knowing everywhere surpasses what God brings forth; thus what God accomplishes[124] lags behind God's knowing and precisely thereby God becomes like one of us.[125] Indeed God becomes much more like one of us than one imagines at first glance, for if we are then able to get a notion of how it is that God would know of what God has not accomplished we would inevitably get into the uttermost anthropomorphism possible. Moreover, the other way around if certain things follow, namely, the condemnation of persons not of faith, which God has not willed, God's will would then definitely be limited, and God would have to be limited. Something viewed as limiting God would stand over and against God. Hence we would inevitably arrive at total Manichaeism no matter whether that opposing principle exists within or outside a human being. Thus, I cannot take part in this moderating expedient. Moreover, although if only in a limited way, some among the Reformed have taken part in this expedient by making a distinction between an actual divine predestination and one which is not actual,[126] I have no wish on this account to justify this move nor to absolve them every inconsistency. This is so, for here everything must be equally actual,[127] because this is a doctrine that can be maintained only in its strictest rigor. For this reason I can also do nothing but commend Calvin for not wanting to grant any validity whatsoever within the domain of scholarly doctrine to the distinction between divine predestination and divine permission, which is generally heard in the language of everyday life and edification.[128] This is so, for what God would merely permit must have its final, positive basis of determination elsewhere. Now, if the opposing principle lies within another person whom God has predestined, the principle would indeed be actually predestined together with this person. In contrast, if it is not within such a person, it would also be placed outside the divine will, and then that permission would be either only a poorly disguised denial of the divine omnipotence or, if it is to be understood as a not-wanting-to-impede,[129] it would revert back, in turn, from another side to become predestination, and the power which is not impeded would itself nevertheless be made dependent on the divine ordering.[130]

For this reason we would confidently abandon this distinction, which in fact functions only to conceal and to bring nothing to light. In plain language we boldly state that if a person who has heard the Word nevertheless dies before faith has been made effective in this person, then this is not simply a matter of God's permission but is rather a matter of God's foreseeing, which by this means calls to everyone: "O that today you would hearken to my voice! Harden not your hearts."[131] Just as when the wickedness that nonetheless already exists in an individual human being, after it has lain inwardly hidden for a long time, at once suddenly breaks forth in all kinds of terrible deeds, this too is not simply a matter of God's permission. It is also a matter of God's predestination, whereby that wickedness might come into the light to be tested by what is good, for otherwise it cannot be overcome.[132] Indeed, even the wickedness that exists in human nature on account of the fall and that increases more intensely in some human beings so that they do ill in the presence of others but increases less in others, so that they look better, this too is not simply a matter of God's permission but is also a matter of God's predestination, because only with regard to these differences can the full extent of wickedness be perceived and can a proper knowledge of sin thus arise. Moreover, because this is all a continual preparation for redemption, I consider it to be a matter not simply of God's permission but rather of God's predestination, lest someone should come and ask me the old question: "If all of this were taken to be simply a matter of God's permission whereby God promotes the work of redemption, would it not then be the case that redemption itself would also be simply a matter of God's permission[133] as well, since it too could not indeed have come into being without someone's being lost in the meantime?" Further, would I seriously want to offer this position in such a way that redemption would have had two appointed and successive causes, first God, who sent Christ according to God's decree, and then Judas, without whom the divine decree would not have reached its goal had he not actually betrayed Christ—not according to God's decree and predestination but according to God's permission? At this point I would fear falling into Manichaeism if my questioner were to go further still and shout at me that I should at the very least be ashamed to stop at Judas but would rather have to go back in turn, to the devil. At that point, quite naturally, that which in God is mere permission is the devil's predestination. Moreover, I would have no option whatsoever but to concede, in the end, that what would have been God's predestination would be precisely permission in the devil.

Moreover, it is exactly this major point that is so frequently overlooked in this controversy, namely, that the strict Augustinian and Calvinian doctrine is made up of two equally essential features of Christian piety. The much discussed anti-Pelagian aspect is, of course, based on the fact that the Christian can have no genuine and joyful consciousness of anything good if one does not regard it as shown to be a gift of God for the sake of Christ. Should a person ever attribute it to oneself, one would feel that the full communion of one's very existence with God would be immediately destroyed. Just as important, however, is the anti-Manichaean aspect that has already been noted, though not so clearly defined or generally acknowledged. This aspect rests on the view that there can be no genuine and joyful feeling for the divine omnipotence if all things are not in the same manner grounded in the one and indivisible, eternal and perfect will and decree of God. It also rests on the view that as soon as one in any way excludes anything from the divine will, a change from one position to the other occurs in which, left without hope, one feels that one is placed under the power of and in communion with yet another will and indeed one that is opposed to the will of God.

Now, what equally emerges from both of these supposedly basic Christian feelings would also—since every Christian truth would deny and exclude self-sufficiency of any human being, on the one hand, and the inadequacy of God, on the other—have necessarily to be in agreement with all Christian truth. Rightly understood, nothing could also follow from these that would require any sort of a moderation[134] of the Christian heart and mind.[135] Therefore, before I assume any moderation that would obscure, even only to some extent, the congruity of these two basic pillars I would prefer to grant the following point: namely, that if some persons, no matter how many or how few, will actually be condemned, this too would not be a matter of mere permission; rather, just as others would be forgiven[136] it would be a matter of God's preordaining[137] and predestination.[138] Moreover, I would simply ask whether the Lutheran church would nonetheless also assume that some persons are lost and would consider this assumption to be compatible with the fatherly love of God, whereby in order to let all persons exist as free beings God established the possibility that by their freedom some persons could be led to destruction? Would the Lutheran church consider it to be compatible with the omnipotence of God that God would have allowed the actuality—if it nevertheless assumes this point then rejects the pure and strict expression of the doctrine for the sake of consequences that were not yet averted previously—that the blessedness of the one and the condemnation of the other would be divine predestination in the same measure and in the same manner? That is to say, we certainly do not want to attach much importance to the claim that scripture itself avoids transferring the term predestination to the disadvantaged side, for this is nevertheless not at all what the Word is dealing with there; rather, it is concerned with what harmoniously proceeds from the omnipotent, and so also, irresistible will of God.[139]

ELECTION AND THE FALL

Now, the next matter to be settled might be this: that if the condemnation of some would be grounded in the divine predestination and the wickedness that leads them to condemnation would be grounded in the fall, then the fall too would have to be grounded in the divine predestination and thus Adam would be destined to fall. Calvin does not deny this implication, and in the strictest terms he refuses to allow that here one might find support in the notion of permission.[140] In fact, moreover, not only can one apply to Adam's first sin what has been stated above, namely, that the not-willing-to-prevent an outcome is in God necessarily a definite willing of this outcome. Rather, the more the entire condition of the human race, in its need for redemption at which all the leadings of God's providence are aimed, is traced back to Adam, as Calvin also does, the less is one able to be persuaded that its fall would not have been predestined by God. This is so, in that otherwise all actual and acknowledged divine determination and ordering within the human world would depend on this event, which would itself have been merely a matter of permission and thus the divine omnipotence in all its expressions would have been determined originally either by human freedom or by intervention of the devil.

Thus, I cannot possibly do otherwise than also to concur with Calvin in this matter too, although I would not want to say as he did, that Adam as Adam was destined to fall; but, rather, I would want to say that it was on account of the fact that the human race was destined to sinfulness and to redemption that Adam became the Adam who was to fall. Moreover, I would further deviate a bit from Calvin with regard to how this view should be explained. That is to say, Calvin certainly was of the opinion that Adam's not being able to sin would have been inherent in his nature, and that he fell so readily because the gift of perseverance would have been denied him, given the tractability of his will for taking one direction or another.[141] However, it does seem to me that it amounts to much the same thing to say that resistance was denied him and to say that he did not possess a definite ability not to sin and that one could come off more easily if one were to say that prior to Christ human nature in general would have possessed neither the capacity to resist nor the ability not to sin. Moreover, this does much to resolve the matter at issue here in that it is easier to account for the way in which God created a human nature that, as it were, would first come to completion through a second creation than to assume that God in fact created in its first exemplars a better nature but willed that thereafter they would change for the worse. The reason is that we can easily dispense with the supposed benefit of contemplating the perfection of human nature in a firmly established and prolonged condition on Adam's part. This is so since in the condition of Adam, who is ever obscure to us, human nature never comes into view with such clarity as it does in that of Christ, who is always clear to us. On the other hand, this matter can be understood much better if one takes as true in general what Calvin says, namely, "A nature that was granted the ability not to sin would indeed have been the more excellent, but the human being has no right to demand of God that God should have made one so;"[142] and also what Augustine says,[143] namely, "The human being stands at a stage of existence such that it is to be made manifest that once free will has first produced the work of sin, divine grace is still able to produce its own work thereafter."

In contrast, I believe this latter take on the matter to be completely sufficient. Moreover, if we are but convinced that such a nature would constitute part of the totality of the finite world, at that point we can also confidently say that as far as it would actually have developed, it was predestined and preordained by God, and there is no need for us to escape into an obscure and unintelligible distinction in God between ordering and permitting.

ELECTION, THE *ABSOLUTUM DECRETUM,* AND CREATION

Now, the second reason why most people want to have such a moderating distinction and do not wish to assume that condemnation of the unrepentant and forgiveness[144] of believers are in the same way ordained by God is because they are of the opinion that it would only be on account of a groundless arbitrariness in God that God would then ordain precisely the latter to blessedness and the former to damnation and not vice versa. Now, here I would note first of all that no one can declare oneself more strongly opposed to such an arbitrariness than Calvin himself,[145] in that the expression for the divine decree of election described as an *absolutum decretum*—an expression that is very misleading, to be sure, but is nonetheless also open to having a very exact interpretation—is not to be found in the *Institutes* but is one that first emerged in controversy. Hence, even the Confession of Sigismund (*Brandenb. Reform. Werk* p. 13) rejects this expression.[146] Instead, Calvin simply states that God would elect and reject at God's own discretion,[147] the grounds for which are unknown to us, that it is a matter of divine decision (*arbitrii*), and that election occurs without regard to human merit.

Now, this latter point is indeed also acknowledged by teachers of the Lutheran church, namely, that even if God would elect only those whose faith God foresees it is nevertheless not on account of that foreseen faith that God would be moved to do so.[148] Now, if it is God who must still actually grant faith, and if the preaching from which that faith alone can arise cannot be made available to everyone under the same favorable circumstances, what is left other than such an act of discretion? However, as Calvin understands it, if we simply think of this act of discretion as having its beginning not in the middle of time but as from the very outset onward, and if we simply do not trace it further out than up to the point where something still really exists about which to inquire about and to establish, then it cannot strike anyone as absurd, or outrageous, or for that matter, groundless. That is, once we are agreed that if the world were to be complete the human race would also have had to exist, we cannot possibly say any longer that it is in groundless arbitrariness that God created the human race, even though God foresaw that it would sin and fall, since creating the human race would, indeed, be necessarily included in the one all-embracing divine act of creating the world. However, if we ask why God created us specifically to be human beings and not to be angels and then want to complain about an unfounded arbitrariness on this account, let us not forget that we could just as well ask why God made us to be human beings and not animals and that we would in that case have to rejoice in the unfounded arbitrariness that we were wanting to complain about. What is more, we would in fact be toying with the question to such an extent that nothing more is to be asked, and thus, strictly speaking, would also not really be questioning at all. That is to say, our selfhood does indeed depend on nothing other than human nature and on the special way in which it is determined in the person of each of us, and if we had not been created to be human beings, we would not actually have been created at all.

This being so, we also have to say that if the human race is to be complete, then for the sake of what is good, more and less receptive persons from all levels at all stages must exist side by side. This is necessary because that completeness in which alone the species actually consists emerges only out of the interconnection of all possible complex conditions of greater and lesser capacities and aptitudes and out of the availability of all possible stages of development and degrees of saturation. Accordingly, presupposing the necessity of the human race, we can in no respect say any longer that it is due to an unfounded arbitrariness that God created all these different persons side by side. However, if we ask why God created certain persons to be less gifted and others to be more gifted, and not vice versa, then again we actually raise no question at all, for if the situation were reversed, the latter would be the former and the former the latter, and nothing would be changed. Therefore, nothing would then be more strange than if, in order to undo this appearance of arbitrariness in God and at the same time to preserve the freedom of human beings, which seems to be threatened on account of these differences that God has ordained, one should rather choose to assume that God would originally have created all persons the same. Under this supposition, despite all obstacles and without any external assistance, every person would be capable of developing all that is good and beautiful in oneself in the same way as anyone else except that this would be something that the one person does but not another. This would be claimed for the human, however, in a most inconceivable manner and in a way that is destructive of the whole idea of the world. The unfounded arbitrariness of God would then be placed within a creature, and if it were anything at all, it would indeed be that "unrestricted freedom which is incompatible with the nature of a creature."[149] Thus, if a person can only be who one is and not someone else, one would be nothing at all if not who one is. Since it is meaningless to ask why God has made someone to be this person and not to be another person, for that reason it also cannot be said that it is on account of an unfounded arbitrariness in God that each person is who one is.

It will be objected, however, that this account would be more a justification of the original spiritual and bodily distinction between persons than of any religious distinction. According to the accepted presupposition—though with the exception of the first parents—a religious distinction would not be an original distinction in the case of all other persons, in that they all would indeed have come to have the same status, on account of the fall. Rather, the objector continues, the distinction would then have first arisen in accordance with that divine decision which grants faith to the one person but not to another and advances the opinion that it is this very decision that appears to be an unfounded arbitrariness. Now the orthodox Lutheran church accepts, as does the Reformed church, the same common identity after the fall, the same necessity for divine constancy, and the same disparity in what God offers. If, as a direct result of everything that has been stated, this objection concerning religious distinctions cannot be made against the Lutheran church—and here it is more a matter of defending the teaching that they hold in common rather than exclusively the Calvinian teaching—admittedly it is nevertheless precisely on the basis of the strength or weakness of this last objection that a decision must be made as to whether the strict Augustinian doctrine can stand the test, or whether one must search for another resource. If the latter, it is preferably one that is more adequate than that which yields people's being divinely predestined on account of a faith that is foreseen.

Now, suppose that we proceed on the basis of the teaching that these churches hold in common, namely, that in the state of sinfulness after the fall no human being has any capacity of one's own to know, to love, or to trust God, or as it is also expressed, that without detriment to one's otherwise having free will for these purposes one would lack this free will.[150] It is thereby clearly implied that, since it is by one's free will that anyone is a religious person, in one's sinning, a human being is indeed in every other respect a person but in a religious respect is not. It is clear that both of these statements are actually synonymous. This is so, for it would be futile for us to search after any other criterion[151] for free will, or, as I would prefer to say, for the will of a human being, for a will that is not free is inconceivable.[152] Rather, the will of the human being operates to this extent, not as spiritual transformations happen to a person, for this can also occur against one's will, but as they emerge[153] out of a person who is involved in a process of spiritual self-development. That is to say, just as the life of any particular thing rests on its being involved in at least a material process of self-development, so too the personal existence or individual spiritual life, viewed as elevated above the non-conscious lower life of plants as well as above the already conscious higher life of animals, does not then rest on spiritual changes happening to the individual being but rather on the fact that these changes are emerging out of oneself and on the fact that one is involved in such a process of self-development. In contrast, a mineral is indeed a part of life in general, in the sense that, viewed in itself alone, it is taken up into the self-development of the earth. Yet precisely because from the moment of its crystallization up to its complete destruction, it is also involved in changes of the kind that simply happen to it and not of the kind that would emerge out of it but rather of the kind that would emerge out of some other source, so it is thought of not as living but as dead. Moreover, the old saying that the sinful person is spiritually "dead" means nothing other than that one is not evolved in the self-development of a conscious relationship to God. On this account the expression can be applied even to persons in whom pious stirrings do occur, yet only on the presupposition that these stirrings are effected in them from outside and do not emerge as self-activated from within them. Furthermore, this saying states nothing other than the teaching presented in the Augsburg Confession[154] that apart from the divine Spirit a human being would have no freedom with regard to spiritual things, for when one has freedom one is also a person and vice versa.

Suppose, however, that someone should want to say that it would be a strange, obscure, confused, or even mystical way of speaking to say that in one respect a human being could be a person and in another respect not; and yet that one who would in fact be a person would be so completely and in every respect. I choose to begin not by referring such an objector to teachers of law but by simply indicating how this usage is understood in everyday life. Who, then, is it whom we call a moral or well-rounded[155] person if not a being who wills and who in the partial surrender of freedom and self-determination is thus also grounded in one's own personal existence as an individual? That is to say, in that sphere in which one individual together with a number of others forms just such a person in common,[156] one is for this reason not then a person in oneself alone, and anyone who chooses to treat a given individual as a singular person will have in mind that larger person as well. Moreover, just as one can to some extent surrender one's personal existence in order to be incorporated with others into such a whole and yet still retain one's personal existence, it must likewise also be possible to possess one's personal existence from the outset only in a partial way, as do children and those held in bondage, who do not yet, as such, have an entirely personal existence but only a partial one. The latter group can be persons especially in the religious sense, whereas they are not yet so in the civic sense but must first be born into this status through emancipation.

Thus, according to this teaching the sinful human being is taken up into the common spiritual life of the human race to the extent that such exists, that is, to the extent that the divine Spirit always brings about such an individual life in certain individuals. These individuals then also exert an influence on others with the result that notions of God and susceptibilities for God are, in turn, transiently produced in them. However, these are not the result of their own action and in consequence are not involved in any self-development of a religious sort but only reflect back that which touches and gets into them from the general life of religion. In the religious sense, however, they are not yet persons but first become such through rebirth when the Holy Spirit will have brought about faith in them. On account of this process, this very transformation is called "regeneration" because in this sphere it is the beginning of one's own individual life of freedom.[157] This is effected, however, by means of the Holy Spirit's bringing forth faith, by virtue of which a human being is incorporated into Christ from whom one receives that higher life and takes it up into oneself. The sole source of this life is Christ,[158] and the former human being does not oneself actually live in that source but rather bears the living Christ in oneself.[159] Prior to regeneration, however, in contrast to those who are regenerated, they are collectively the "dead," the mere mass—an expression which therefore appears so frequently in Augustine and Calvin[160]—which dead mass is capable of being quickened and also of which certain particular points are quickened by the Spirit at work in and through people who have already been quickened.

Thus, those who are quickened—that is, those in whom religious self-development arises at each new beginning of life in a marked, yet inexplicable way—comprise the elect. Furthermore, just as we believe that no human being, once one has become a person, actually ceases to be one and just as that in so believing we accord this special status to any individual human being possessed of spirit, likewise of these latter individuals we also believe, that as long as no mere semblance of life has deceived us, once they have become persons in the religious sense they too will never cease to be such.

In contrast, the remainder of the mass—who have not been warmed up to their proper life and who, even though they never cease to be taken up into the common religious life and for this reason also do not, viewed of themselves, forfeit the possibility in and for themselves of also being quickened, to the extent that they are not quickened—comprise the condemned. These people can actually be called the condemned only if one takes into consideration the personal existence that falls to them within the sphere of the human life shared in common. Now, suppose that we want to demand some reason for the fact that from this collective mass God lets some portions[161] be quickened and not others. We can do so only with the same justification as that with which we could also demand some reason for the fact that, from the totality of all human embryos, God quickens some and lets them become persons and others not, rather leaving them as they are in a state of non-personhood[162] and death, really leading some into the light of day, but returning again to death others already in the womb or immediately at birth.

CREATION AND REDEMPTION PRESUME ONE DIVINE DECREE

Thus, on the basis of such a thoroughgoing examination, divine arbitrariness in election and nonelection appears to be in no respect different or greater than that in creation. At the same time light is also shed upon the sense in which it is indeed quite right that one cannot regard condemnation to be a positive divine decree, just as surely as no one yet has ever regarded it to be a positive divine decree that this or that would not have been created. In contrast, it is then also not right, in turn, to want to take election of individual human persons to be a special decree and the condemnation of other individuals not to be such. Rather, the one must hold true in the same sense as the other does. The truth of the matter, however, is that only *one* divine decree can be assumed, one that embraces all, namely, the decree concerning that arrangement within which those of the mass who are capable of individual spiritual life are gradually quickened. As soon as this point of view has been grasped, it must be clear to anyone that in the sphere of this spiritual creation the motives[163] of the divine will are no more to be sought in how it will be constituted in the future, which will be as it is to be only through this actual creation, than we should seek or wish to seek to discover those motives in the sphere of creation in general and not rather trace the constitution and destiny of individual things only to the *one* general act of creation by the divine omnipotence.

Moreover, if one should nevertheless want merely to search for the divine motives regarding this or that specific thing, to this extent I cannot do otherwise than take Calvin to be right in not wanting to go beyond the divine will, which is itself the divine justice. Indeed, it seems almost strange if one seeks to disparage the all-determining will of God as blind and groundless arbitrariness because will is itself not determined by something particular. However, this appearance of blind arbitrariness, against which Calvin so urgently and earnestly protests, largely arose from that scholastic method, which raised specific questions torn out of context[164] and did so in such a way that it is not often noticed how the entire presupposition is thereby destroyed. As a result of that method the questions raised could not be resolved. This method has introduced well-nigh impenetrable confusion into almost every important point in the Christian body of doctrine. Together with all that it has produced this scholastic method cannot be banished too strongly, for the purpose that this era, along with the superficial resistance to it, can finally be closed and a new treatment of faith-doctrine[165] developed that leaves no room for such questions but completely rejects them.

For example, if it is asked whether according to the Calvinian doctrine anyone predestined to blessedness by God must thus be blessed, even if this person should yield to every vice and live in the most outrageous unbelief, the presupposition that divine predestination is bound up with bringing about faith has in large part been forgotten. However, the fact that, by means of divine grace, faith can also be brought about in someone who lives in obvious unbelief and vice is something that the Lutheran church has never denied. Calvin answers the question as follows, namely, that if a consistent and well-founded faith could still be brought about even in someone who is unbelieving and wicked, such a person would be predestined to salvation at the extraordinary cost of the divine mercy. The Lutheran church would not take exception to this other than to add its point that such a person would be predestined with regard to the faith that God has foreseen,[166] whereas Calvin, on the other hand, would stick with his own point that such a person would have come to faith because God has intended for this person a sufficient measure of the operations of grace. However, the fact that one could have been wicked and unbelieving in the highest degree, and yet be preordained, must indeed be granted all the more, the more one insists on the universality of divine grace in Christ.

Moreover, if the question is posed the other way around and it is asked regarding anyone who is preordained to damnation whether such a one must be damned even if living a most virtuous life, with the orthodox parties of both churches I would answer that indeed in no respect is any person saved on account of one's works[167] but is saved by faith, and that we know of no predestination in accordance with which any person of faith can be lost.[168] However, the claim that a person who, in spite of an outwardly irreproachable life, and who would nevertheless not have attained to faith, would also not have been predestined by God to the blessedness of faith—supported by the view that faith cannot ever be earned by means of works, and that on account of outward appearances we can deem many to be persons of faith when they really are not—this is also granted by the orthodox party of the Lutheran church. Moreover, the sense in which it is to be said of such a person that one would simply not be elect, as well as the sense in which that person would be condemned and predestined to condemnation, are matters that have already been discussed above.

Thus, almost all of these issues have this stamp, with the result that there is no need to delay ourselves any further over others. Once one simply faces them directly and understands them properly, they are not at all intimidating; rather, on their account the matter can stay just as it was. The situation stands no better with the reproach that Reinhard has brought up in turn, namely, "It is of course a slanderous rebuke when of a person's decisions it would have to be said: *stat pro ratione voluntas*[169] and, according to this claim the reckless Thor would be the most similar to the deity, the prudent sage the least similar."[170] That is to say, it would surely remain reproachful for the person who always simply carries on with one's existence through one's own actions and to whom some gift is always being offered, if such a one were not to connect with what is given to oneself as a gift. God, however, simply cannot be a sage after the manner of human beings, because nothing is ever given to God and because it is God who always originates all things. For that reason one certainly cannot think of any divine decree as consequent upon something else but can think of it only as preceding all things. How then can it be said, moreover, that with regard to election God should take into consideration how human beings are constituted? Humans are not indeed conditioned apart from God but first receive conditioning by means of the same indivisible divine decree in which election is also included. To this extent, it must indeed be called unconditional since it is the decree itself that first conditions all things. Moreover, faith, being foreseen is also conditioned in this way. This is so, for faith is nothing other than the consequence of something given. In fact, it is also determined as a result of the divine decree's conditioning it in precisely this way and not otherwise. Even a personal existence that is mentally dead is conditioned, however, by a certain potency in the working of grace that is still dependent on divine predestination. Thus, the will to create cannot be defined by reasons in the manner that the mere will to influence must be defined. Hence, the appearance of blasphemy, namely, that the same thing should be ascribed to God as that for which a human being would be rebuked, dissolves into nothing, for the same thing is not asserted in that case but something entirely different.

ELECTION, THE AUTHORSHIP OF EVIL, AND THE CAPTIVITY OF REASON

Thus, if equal consideration is given to the two aspects of this doctrine, the anti-Pelagian and the anti-Manichaean, and if in addition one takes into account the entirely scriptural understanding of the new spiritual creation through Christ and his Spirit—one, however, that is seldom sufficiently illuminated—this much indeed seems to become clear, namely, that not only is the strict Augustinian/Calvinian doctrine alone entirely in keeping with the presupposition of human incapacity apart from Christ and his Spirit, but also that, on closer examination, most of the objections raised against it disappear. Only two objections seem still to remain among those, which even Dr. Bretschneider raises in particular. On account of their special character, I did not make any reference to them in the above discussion but would wish to subsume them within yet another special investigation. The first objection is this: if the predestination of the human race to fall into sin can by no means be denied, then it is incomprehensible that, according to Calvin's doctrine, God should not be understood to be the author of sin. The second objection is that this Calvinian doctrine would completely cut off any attempt to fathom the depths of the divine decree and that precisely by this means reason, which strives ever more broadly and deeper, would be held in an intolerable captivity.

Now, as far as the first objection is concerned in no way do I deny it. According to my conviction, although in his presentation of the doctrine, Calvin did succeed in avoiding everything Manichaean and everywhere demonstrated the omnipotence of God in the same unclouded light, he was not so successful as to offer a clear explication of the fact that irrespective of predestination God would not be the author of human evil. Rather, in this respect too he always had to revert to the alternative view. Nevertheless, I should like immediately to ask where, then, could there be a clear explication in connection with the Lutheran theory as to how God is not the author of human evil irrespective of the fact the God willed that the human will should be free and created it so and foreknew that it would be the source of sin? Granted, Augustine and Calvin do set forth the oft-repeated assertion that Satan too has drawn to himself everything that is to be condemned and also that human beings have plunged themselves into disaster.[171] They deny frequently and definitely enough that God is in any respect the author of sin in general or of particular offenses. However, I do not want to maintain that Calvin was completely successful in making clear the sense in which this would not be the case since everything that is real is nonetheless to be traced to the divine omnipotence. Yet, from the other perspective I am also aware of no other assertion than precisely this same one, namely, that the final cause[172] of human evil is to be found in the freedom of the finite human will. However, it has never been made clear to me how, on the basis of this assertion, God would be exempt from being the author of evil since, after all, God is the author of freedom. That is to say, if God had definitely and unconditionally willed that there would be no human evil, the whole constitution of the world and of spiritual beings within it would have to have conformed to this will and the world would have become something different. Now, given that it is such a world, and supposing that God would also simply have foreknown and permitted the use of freedom from which human evil arose and would have ordered the whole world in advance on the presupposition that human evil would become a reality, then God patently would not have willed that evil should not exist. As a consequence, the difference between the two views would, in turn, be none other than that between an unqualified predestination and a predestination admixed with permission, a difference that at the finite, human sphere of a purely elective will certainly counts for something but that in the divine sphere of a creative will means nothing. Such is the case, for the familiar adage that misuse of freedom would be better than no freedom at all cannot be satisfactory, because the lack in omnipotence involved cannot be expressed more clearly than in terms of the necessity of choosing the lesser of two evils.

Thus, on this point the two theories are equally deficient. Moreover, suppose that something could still be done to resolve the issue more straightforwardly and clearly as to how it is that if nothing is in any sense excluded from the creative will of God, God would then still not be the author of evil. Then both theories would necessarily turn out to be of some advantage. Furthermore, if the one party could make some progress in this matter that the other party might not be able to acknowledge on account of its own divergent formulation, only then would an advantage be attributed to the one over the other in this respect. However, it is sufficiently clear to me that there can be no other and more precise solution to this problem than this one solution that is common to both parties. This is so, for once it is stated that if everything that is real would have to be established by the creative will of God and then, on the other hand, that God could not be the author of human evil, then indeed these two statements are to be reconciled in only one way, namely, only if one can say that in relation to God, human evil does not exist at all. Yet, this unavoidable formula—however one might then resolve it as one chooses and might continually attempt to explain it in whatever manner—states how human evil could exist for us in such a way that it exists neither through God nor for God. This it claims in such a way that this free and effective sense-oriented power is that of which God cannot not be the author. However, that of which God cannot be the author,—namely, the opposite of what is good—really does not exist. However, the necessity for redemption rests on that which really exists, and, at the same time this necessity passes from that of which God could not be the author, into that of which God alone can be the author, namely, into what is good.

As I say, this formula can in no way whatsoever be entangled with that difference between God's permission and God's predestination, which we have been discussing. Moreover, the resolution of that difference, if one is to be found at all, must be able to be adopted by both doctrinal opinions. Suppose, however, that it really has been truly demonstrated that God is not the author of human evil, and in a way that is indeed also in agreement with the teaching of scripture that apart from the law there is no sin.[173] Then we would have to say that the most important reason for accepting any distinction between God's permission and God's predestination would also fall away of itself. As a result, at that point everyone would find themselves in agreement with Calvin on this matter, just as on the other hand, at that point it would also make sense to say that human evil is not predestined by God, precisely because in fact it does not exist. Thus, if this problem can be solved, the difference of opinions between the two churches on this topic would altogether disappear of itself.

Now, with regard to the second objection, namely, that the Calvinian doctrine completely prevents reason from penetrating the mystery of the divine decree in that it straightaway sets forth an unfathomable discretion in it, I refer, first of all, to what has already been stated, namely, that the doctrine of the Lutheran church as it is set forth in the Formula of Concord[174] does precisely the same thing, even though it does not set forth the formulation of such a divine discretion straightaway and does not admit so unqualifiedly as does Calvin that we could not possibly go beyond the divine will. However, let no one say that here I appeal to the Formula of Concord yet elsewhere—when it most diverges from the Calvinian doctrine—that I appeal, in turn, to the fact that the Formula of Concord is not acknowledged as a symbolic book by the whole Lutheran church! Rather, I find these statements, already expressed above together with doctrines expounded in the Augsburg Confession on human incapacity and on the way in which faith is brought about, to be closely interconnected. In fact, Dr. Bretschneider also takes the entire Calvinian doctrine to consist in a chain of strict conclusions arising from that presupposition that we have been discussing.

Before we go much further, however, I should like to raise the following question. With regard to the complaint of reason, namely, that here in the sphere of divine predestination to blessedness through faith, reason is nonetheless prevented from fulfilling its proper role and from pursuing the direction in which it feels itself to be irresistibly driven, I want to ask this: If that complaint is to have any basis and if it is to be heard, would reason not first have to demonstrate to us that it would be more successful in fathoming the divine decrees at some other point? That is to say, if reason should fail to succeed at other points as well, and if reason everywhere has to be stilled, why, then, does it want to raise a special complaint here? I do not believe, however, that it has gained more ground elsewhere either in the domain of history or in the domain of nature. This is so, for if we likewise ask concerning the individual as to why God happens to bestow this or that gift on this or that person and denies it to others— which amounts to the same as asking why God has placed such and such a person precisely in this place and at this time and not in another—this, I believe, reason will never know. Moreover, is reason to inform us as to why there should be deserts on this place on earth and a high range of mountains on that place and not vice versa? This too, I believe, reason will not know. Moreover, it is of no help to reason if it chooses to hide behind effective causes in regard to the divine decree, because there are effective causes in those other areas too. Effective causes are also ordained by God in every area, however, and the question that arises is precisely why God has ordered them in such a way that they bring about precisely these effects and not others. Thus, if reason can never find further grounds for the determination of divine decrees elsewhere, why exactly should it nevertheless want to know why it is that God grants faith to one person and not to another? Moreover, if reason does not gain this insight within the entire domain of history, what sort of basis do we have for surrendering the presupposition of human incapacity together with its acknowledged consequences so that reason would gain this insight in the religious domain? That is to say, making this surrender could still gain nothing more than that the religious domain would be treated on entirely equal terms with the rest of history. I believe, therefore, that if reason is to take the wisest course in dealing with final causes within the religious domain as with the whole domain of nature, since it must precisely on account of its weakness first separate the two causes, it should leave them alone, and apply itself to information regarding effective causes. It is with regard to these effective causes that reason is certain to discover glorification of the divine wisdom. On the one hand, it explores the multiplicity of ways in which the divine Spirit acts upon the most hardened hearts and minds and gradually transforms them, and, on the other hand, it also explores how even good-natured souls nevertheless do fall behind and fail to attain any real inner peace if they are left without proper address from the divine Word. Moreover, in these inquiries reason does not have to stop at matters in general but can always inquire into the details. Thereby everything must be instructive for the very person who is and wants to be an instrument of the divine Spirit in spreading faith so that one can learn how each soul is best to be directly treated and cultivated and how to distinguish between the perceptible alternations of favorable and blessed times and those that seem to be barren and can perhaps only be further prepared.

However, if reason cannot content itself in this fashion, as it seeks to experience in ever more detail and ever more precisely how the reign of God is present and will be so, and if it cannot refrain from asking about the why and wherefore, then reason itself would simply acknowledge the extent to which it is qualified elsewhere and how in fact it is nevertheless driven back ever again from final causes to effective causes. That is to say, if reason pursues what is of a general nature, it thereby commits itself to optimism or to the rule of what is best, namely, that everything in the world is so and happens for the best. However, even there it is very difficult to say what the best is, and if one inadequate formula should be designated as definitive, it always tends to displace another one. More-over, it is even more difficult to exhibit how some particular detail coop-erates with and contributes to this best, with the result that this particular detail could not have been attained if that particular detail had been other than it is. Still, this much always remains certain, that the best is simply that which includes nothing apart from the best, the result being that with regard to any particular detail, one is thus not driven to the question of its end and purpose; rather, each detail bears its end within itself. At that point, moreover, the only question that remains is that regarding the interconnectedness of all the particulars among themselves and with the oneness of the whole, which is the question not of the wherefore but of the how.

However, suppose we begin this inquiry from the particular and ask, nevertheless, whether this or that, whether it is then good or bad, would it have had to be exactly so and not otherwise? Consider how seldom we will also be able to give an account even such that such a particular detail would have to be exactly as it is in order that this or that could follow from it! Yet, suppose that we even believe that we see such a matter as this ever so clearly. Then the question reappears nonetheless since this matter too is merely something of a particular nature and the question as to why this matter too had to be exactly as it is and not otherwise and neither sooner nor later, and there certainly can be no rest from our labors until we have arrived at the idea of a general interconnectedness in which each particular is both active and at the same time in a process of becoming. Thus, the only question that can be posed concerns the place and signifi-cance of each particular in the whole. This is the situation in every case, and here too the situation can be no different, and neither the one theory nor the other nor indeed even the third more recent one makes any dif-ference. Suppose that someone asks why one person is received into the reign of God and not another. I certainly know of nothing else to say than to answer with Calvin: only because God has willed it to be so. Moreover, by this response we mean nothing other than that this particular detail too is not at all arbitrarily thrown into the mix; rather, it is destined along with the general interconnection to be both what and how God has ordained—but not in and of itself nor in reference to any particularity whatsoever.

The fact that the Lutheran church also knows no more than this arises from statements in the Formula of Concord cited above.[175] Moreover, no form of Pelagian theory—if it does not postulate that absolute freedom, which, as far as its influence extends, always simply destroys the omnipo-tence of God entirely—would be able to make any further progress than this. However, the salutary retreat from the pointless question about the motives of the divine will to the highly instructive question about its narrower specificity does mostly alleviate the strictness of the Calvinian theory. This is so, first of all, because the latter question does not want to go behind the divine will, and we are always in a position to examine most precisely that with which we are able to linger. Further, the latter question alleviates the strictness of the Calvinian theory even more because it most definitely holds that on account of the fact that God's elective decree, because it generates spiritual life out of the unspiritual life, is a creative divine will. It is creative in that it brings forth a world that exists in measure and order and is itself to be viewed as a power that acts in accordance with measure and order. However, the task is to understand this power ever more precisely in the way it works and in its laws. This is a task that we ought not to prevent human reason, as illuminated by God's Spirit, from solving, and it is one that the Augustinian theory is far from prohibiting.

Only once we have let go of the particular, wherein the limitless multiplicity of what are for us an unending number of small details, mostly bewildering us, and have, instead of this, broken into contemplating things as a whole, are we convinced—as has already been noted above as being in the fullest possible agreement with the Calvinian theory—that one cannot speak, in particular, of a divine decree concerning each individual person. Rather, we can say that there is only *one* decree by which God determines what will become of each and every human being and thus that this decree is not at all different from the order according to which the dead mass is quickened by the divine Spirit. This result already implies the following: that just as the Word became flesh, an individual human being in Christ, in the same way the Spirit of God was poured out on his disciples and bound with the Word in its working, has become a spiritual power of nature forming individual spiritual beings.[176] Yet, although equally active in and of itself on all sides, this spiritual power of nature was also determined by the diverse levels of need and receptivity that are inherent in the material[177] presented to it. In proceeding from this observation and in exploring in this manner the way the divine Spirit works, we arrive at a procedure that seems to offer the only suitable way to deal with any situation concerning divine action and effect, namely, at that process in which final causes and effective causes converge.

GOD IN ELECTION INTENDS THE WHOLE

Christ himself explained the distinctive character[178] of his work when he says: "I have not come to call the righteous, but sinners to repentance."[179] We surely do not want to understand his aim in a particularistic way. Rather, we want to take it to have exactly the same meaning as the words that immediately precede: "Those who are well have no need of a physician, but those who are sick." Accordingly, a more precise description of his success would be that the call he issued on all sides would have the most powerful effect on those in whom evil and also the feeling of evil had developed most strongly. By the same token, Paul too inquired as to how, despite all else, it should happen that by the Word the Spirit of God would have a more powerful impact on the Gentiles than on the Jews. This observation, moreover, he expressed to all intents and purposes teleologically in this way: "a hardening has come upon part of Israel, until the full number of the Gentiles come in, and so all Israel will be saved."[180] This statement, despite all else, means nothing other than that in comparison with the Jews it was precisely the Gentiles who were sick whereas it was the Jews who were well, and that on the whole, once the Jews would have come to be entirely surrounded by the greater health that the Gentiles had attained through the Gospel, they too would come to a feeling of their sickness. As Origen[181] explains it: "The more pleasing work of the Word is to save those of greater understanding, for these are more similar to the Word than those who are dull-minded," and herewith he also articulates a law of nature in conformity with which the outpoured Spirit acts through the Word and according to which we surely must understand the words with which he continues: "However, due to the fact that the majority of the house of Israel were not those of a true understanding, the Spirit sought out from among that which was foolish to the world, that which was truly wise and similar."

Why, then, should we who see the divine decree so much further developed not inquire concerning this matter in precisely the same way? Thus, linking the particular to the general we shall say, "Once it cannot be denied—because it shows itself to be so—that the human race, viewed as first redeemed from the power of sin through the appearance of the divine Son, belongs to the idea of the world and so holds an indispensable place within it which was foreseen and ordained by God, it also follows that it has been so ordained in its complete totality. Moreover all the different interweavings of human capacities—even in various levels of corruption and weakness where divine things are concerned—must have been developed before Christ, in accordance with the divine decree that grants to each its own place and time." Yet, it was into this diverse profusion of corrupt existence that the divine Spirit then came through Christ, was united with the proclamation of the Word and thereby was made human just as occurred in Christ the Son. In this way, moreover, the spiritual life then arises in accordance with the divine decree just as the natural life does. Likewise, the Christian church, the common bearer of the Word of God, in its working on the mass that is capable of being quickened, now here now there, reaches that very instant, one that precisely on that account was also conditioned by all previous situations and concurrent events. Even down to the seemingly most fortuitously conditioned instant then, events were predestined by God for the new beginning of an individual life, that is, an instant when one's longing for redemption—a good that is never completely to vanish from human nature[182]—opens itself in its full receptivity to the influence of the Spirit. However, when and as long as this working of the Spirit does not encounter such an instant, no new life arises. In contrast, as thereby conditioned and brought to maturity, in turn, and as by all means wrought by God, those moments of the new creation of the future predestined by God, as they are even more widely spread abroad, develop out of the mass of nothingness and corruption the most abundant multiplicity of spiritual life in each case as the Spirit appropriates to itself the diverse natural gifts that human beings have. These are the instants that exhibit the reign of God, which is ever more strengthened in that in every newly quickened person it gains, in turn, a potent instrument of the quickening Spirit, and also all the more easily overcomes resistance. This reign of God, moreover, already by virtue of its more distant influences indeed binds and softens that which strives against it, allowing us a glimpse of that final instant beyond the unknown and unpredictable apportionments[183] of progress, when all the dead will be made alive and every resistance taken up into the oneness of the whole.

Now, this is the manner of the undivided decree of election as well as of rejection: accordingly, those who in this way are taken hold of by the power of the Word are quickened and born again, each as God has ordained one's mode of being and time, and these are "the elect." However, consider those who are not grasped, be it on account of the fact that they were placed by God in an already enlightened circle of persons as those who were the most unreceptive—and who were also not to be excluded—or because they were destined to die before the quickening Word entered into the circle of their lives. We may call these persons, if so desired, either "those overlooked" for whom allowances have been made[184] inasmuch as they do indeed simply demonstrate what the Spirit was not, after all, in a position to achieve, after the measure in which it was active in a given place. Alternatively, they may also be called "the reprobate"[185] inasmuch as in God, after all, foreknowledge and predestination can indeed be only one and the same thing. Moreover, to my mind, Calvin also would have no objection to this attempt to present the distinct resolution[186] of the divine decree for in this way no attempt is made to search for motives of the divine will outside or, as it were, beyond the same. On the contrary, based on this presentation, the creating and ordering divine will remains God's ultimate will,[187] one that is not determined by any consideration of the human being, for mere flesh cannot please God[188] and the Spirit is first imparted through and in accordance with this decree. Rather, only in this way is it to become clear how the election and rejection of individuals are simply the two contrasted yet in each instance correlated aspects of one and the same decree, whereby through divine power, yet in a natural way, the human race is to be transformed into the spiritual body of Christ. Furthermore, just as this decree, viewed in terms of its oneness, is nothing other than a demonstration of divine love, from which Calvin also never wanted to separate the divine will, it is likewise shown—if one reduces it to its contrasted features, that is, considers it in its temporal appearance—precisely in this natural unfolding of the divine will, to be that most just cause of all things that Calvin sought out and everywhere presupposed. Consequently, on this understanding, namely, that the divine Spirit is active through the Word as a power of nature, nothing is included other than simply a more precise statement of the Calvinian "according as it pleases God" (*prout visum est Deo*; *Inst.* 3.21.10). This is indeed the case, for it was indeed God's good pleasure from the beginning not to create individual being and life but to create a world, and this is also the way in which the Spirit of God is active, as a world-forming power, and through the Spirit of God there arises not the disorder of individual spiritual life but the spiritual world.

Now, accordingly, if the entire doctrine is traced back to this formulation in which alone—as has been discussed here—the distinct resolution of the divine will can be perceived, it seems to me that only one thorn still remains, namely, that *horribile*[189] term in the Calvinian decree that those "overlooked" or "the reprobate" are then damned to all eternity and deprived of any blessedness, in spite of the fact that, in accordance with their nature and in accordance with the universal power of redemption, as well, they have the very same claims as the rest. Moreover, there really are no other claims, for the Lutheran church too concedes no other claims than on divine grace. Furthermore, it is precisely this that makes no sense with regard to the eternal fatherly love of God, a topic that to this point we have to some extent sought to conceal and even to avoid, in that we have simply spoken more about the reign of God without especially emphasizing blessedness, and still less have we given thought to the matter of eternal damnation.

Now, as concerns this matter, it is very difficult indeed to think about the topic in an orderly way. However, I would not want to shy away from saying of a person who is damned that he or she might well consider that God could also not have created the person at all yet now the person is nevertheless conscious of existing, or one might well consider that God could have created the person to be a beast, yet now the person is nevertheless conscious of possessing his or her reason. After all, a person must be conscious of one's reason to remain the same as what one was and will be, namely, a human being. It is also true, moreover, since in this consciousness a person compares the self with lesser creatures and with nonbeing,[190] that one must feel that one has no right to demand anything of God. However, whether within this consciousness there is not already lodged a kind of satisfaction that bars access to any absolute misery, or whether reason can exist as consciousness within a person without its also being active and capable of advancing in its activity are matters that I do indeed choose to leave undecided.

Still, be this as it may, it is nevertheless my opinion that also, as far as this matter is concerned, an unjustifiable reproach is brought against the Calvinian theory that would exclude it from consideration. Or is it indeed the case that the difference between divine preordination and permissive divine foreknowledge is so great that if one considers the matter of eternal damnation, only one of these two concepts could fail to be compatible with the universal fatherly love of God, whereas if one were to accept the other, it would then appear in its full light? Should one not rather say, moreover, that the merciful Father would surely not have created those whose eternal damnation God had only foreseen? Or is the difference between the guilt of one who has become a person of faith—since innocence or merit do indeed have nothing to do with the matter—and the guilt of one who has continued not to be a person of faith so great that the infinite difference between blessedness and damnation for all eternity could be justified thereby?

However, I do not choose to repeat such frequent, also mostly superficial statements. Rather, I want first simply to refer back to what I adduced above concerning the relationship of human resistance to divine predestination, which also continually seems to me not to be stated superficially. Second, I simply want to point out that as a consequence of this point, divine justification with regard to damnation of one part of the human race does not at all seem to me to depend upon whether one accepts preordination or foreseeing. Rather, it depends instead upon whether or not one views the condition of the damned as one that would be necessary across the whole range of human nature, a condition given with the very idea of human nature and therefore a condition that is to be fulfilled[191] by certain individuals from among the species. That is to say, in the latter case I know of no way in which it can be reconciled with the universal love of God, no more in the Lutheran theory than in the Calvinian theory, and I think that with respect to the former case as well, no other recourse remains but to go back to the notion of the incomprehensibility and impenetrability of the divine decree. On the other hand, if the condition of the damned were thought to be a necessary stage, then indeed it would be the ordering of the divine justice that fulfills[192] human nature and this we can also always grant to be a predestining justice from which we can subtract nothing. However, it also follows, in part, that because damnation is taken to be a necessary stage, it must also be a stage of development, for in the domain of active spiritual nature the two cannot be separated. It also follows, in part, that the damned likewise cannot be excluded from being objects of divine love since everything that belongs to the ordered world of human life must be an object of all the divine attributes.

Now, suppose that someone wants to say that by this means the theological question is, in turn, transposed into the realm of speculation. Then, let this person simply bear in mind that in no respect was it I who occasioned this move. Rather, it was those who attribute to the Calvinian doctrine its being incompatible with divine mercy, a problem not shared by the Lutheran theory. For all that, it is not at all our intention to delve more deeply into speculation. Rather, on returning immediately to the theological sphere, we want simply to note that as soon as that objection is raised— one much more linked to the fact of damnation than to the way in which one apportions causality between God and human beings with regard to damnation—both parties find themselves at a crossroads. Either they will take the road of accepting an eternity and endlessness of the punishments of hell, together with the incomprehensibility of the divine ordinances; or in order to surmount at the same time any conflict between divine justice and divine love, they turn to the notion of an ultimate universal reconciliation and restoration of all that have been lost. Whichever road is taken, the difference at the point of death, then, between the person of faith and the person not of faith is simply the difference between being taken up into the reign of Christ earlier and later. Along with the idea of a temporal world, this difference is necessarily given in each person in accordance with a conceivable measure of the actual range of that temporal world.

Now, concerning me, I would gladly take the latter road in that it is easier for my feeling to bear not only the thought of people without faith dying but also the thought of those who are already forgiven[193] at this point and of all those who are blessed but for whom blessedness would nevertheless have to be disturbed by the thought of those who have forever been excluded. Alternatively, could they perchance be blessed at all if they would have to lose compassion[194] for everything that belongs to their species? At that juncture, however, it seems to me that this latter notion is as well supported in scripture as is the former notion, which if anything new could be said, still cannot be further enlarged upon here. What is more, the latter, preferable notion can only be brought to a certain degree of clarity, whereas the more closely the former notion is examined, the greater are the difficulties that seem to accumulate. Only in taking this latter route, moreover, does one's understanding find rest, supposing that it is able to consider the original and unfolded diversity of all human beings together with the dependence of all on divine grace, the divine power of redemption together with what can arise from the resistance of human beings, and, finally, the misery of those who have no faith together with the Word of grace that has laid hold of their remembrance. Moreover, in that I would confess to holding this view, I advance it as a sign of my impartiality in not asserting that the Calvinian theory drives us any more strongly to this view than does the Lutheran theory.

Now, if this information about the Calvinian theory, nevertheless, remains just as transparent as many in the Lutheran church have understood it to be all along, and if the person who does not want to grasp the Calvinian theory discovers that the difficulties of reconciling eternal damnation with divine love are just as great in the Lutheran position as in the Calvinian position, it will then seem that in this connection too a Lutheran relaxation of the original long-established strictness of doctrine would be of no essential help. Moreover, if in fact—as I indeed am fully convinced—this strict theory is such an inevitable and rigorous consequence of the anti-Pelagian doctrine of human incapacity as Dr. Bretschneider has stated it to be, then I would only wish that by the way in which I have attempted to settle the objections made against the strict theory—if indeed Dr. Bretschneider himself has perhaps not succeeded in persuading certain others—that for the sake of those harmful consequences, which arise from the strict doctrine of election, it is not necessary to abandon that fundamental Evangelical doctrine of the incapacity of the sinful human being.

ELECTION AND CHURCH UNION

With this wish, moreover, I would now bring my essay to a close if I did not believe I must say a few more words on the matter in connection with union of the two Protestant churches. First of all, I fear that it will be objected that it is very strange that I, who have wished for this union for so long, am bringing this point of doctrine to expression in this way and defending it so persistently. Indeed the prevailing view is that just as many Lutherans had already drawn closer to the Calvinian doctrine of the Lord's Supper, similarly most of the Reformed had already abandoned the Calvinian doctrine of predestination. This latter point I would in no way deny, for there are also many Reformed teachers who, on their part, shrink from the harsh expressions of that doctrine and many of them who, on their part, do not hold all that firmly to the basic doctrine of human incapacity. However, if I allow the latter group of teachers to go their own way as far as they are able to go, and also have sought to reassure the former group of teachers, for the same reason that I am a supporter of the union, I also have just as much at heart members of the Lutheran church. These Lutherans, while adhering to the shared fundamental doctrine of the indispensability of divine help[195]—if indeed it has already been made clear to them from Dr. Bretschneider's *Aphorisms* that this doctrine is wholly consistent and compatible only with the Calvinian doctrine of predestination, whereas the Lutheran doctrine has formed[196] an inconsistency with it—might be inclined to want to get rid of this inconsistency and change over to the Calvinian doctrine, and for these people, I have wanted to ease the transition and thus facilitate unity among themselves. This I have accomplished, in that having presented this doctrine in its clarity, I have sought to free it from the objections that are made against it and to set the harsh expressions in their proper light.

On this account, I have also deliberately refrained from drawing any quotations and justifications from the Synod of Dordrecht.[197] This I have done, for in this confession there are really harsh statements that rather than clarifying the matter in itself only obscure it and that arose only on account of the fact that people there engaged with vacuous skill for disputation questions that were not derived from a clear perception of the matter.

The original presentation in Calvin's *Institutes* kept itself entirely free from such practice, and it is simply this Calvinian presentation that I want to defend and with regard to which it is my wish that this might become the point around which the Evangelical Church would gather. These are my views, for in no respect is it my opinion—though I have been blamed for it—that, notwithstanding the union, I would desire that differences of opinion should continue to exist as though I would want to prevent any possible harmony of opinions. On the contrary, I want that difference to be allowed to continue only if such harmony were not to be achieved. It is also for this reason that I have drawn special attention to the way in which the Formula of Concord deals with this matter. Dr. Bretschneider completely avoided referring to this statement, which is also quite natural since he considers the doctrine of the natural incapacity of human beings with regard to spiritual things to be a point of secondary importance that a Lutheran theologian could easily abandon. In his *Glükkwünschungsschreiben* Dr. Ammon does indeed cite it on page 37,[198] but the densely packed synopsis of its content which he offers is so incomplete that already on this account one cannot praise it for being truly accurate, and no one would imagine that this is what is really stated in the Solid Declaration. However, if this document is compared with Calvin's *Institutes*, one has to view the distinction between actual predestination and foreknowing permission as a distinction that in fact lies beyond the sphere of general information and as unable to exert any influence on life. Moreover, in this same connection one also has to agree with the opinion of the blessed Töllner,[199] one of those theologians who seems to have been too soon forgotten and who without justification is also not cited by Mr. Ammon on this matter but who states, "With regard to the union of the two churches everything depends upon the controversial points being declared to be too lofty,"[200] and thus views this difference as well as that regarding the Lord's Supper as one that belongs only to the academy and not to life. Now, herewith I too have repeatedly held this position, and I take it to be the case and believe it to be entirely feasible that both opinions exist in *one* church. I believe, moreover, that anyone who is imprudent and indiscreet enough to have a harmful influence on the people owing to observations of this sort could do just as well at this by using one opinion as by using the other. However, on this account I would have nothing against it if union could be achieved, but it is of no help to unite if differences of opinion arise repeatedly, and for my own part I believe that this process would most easily be prevented if we were to rally round the long-established Augustinian opinion. This would be appropriate, for no middle view between the ecclesiastical Lutheran theory as it is presented in the *Book of Concord* and the Calvinian theory is to be found. Thus, one must choose the one or the other, and here, it seems to me, is how the matter stands: if one chooses the Lutheran formula, the controversy will always have to revive, because the Lutheran formula bears the germ of conflict in itself, in part because there is no complete agreement on the doctrine of human incapacity and in part because it sets divine and human causality over and against each other in such a way that in the domain of community they have to become separated, even though one does not rightly know how. Hence, again and again this necessarily produces a lack of satisfaction for persons who insist on strict consistency and clear perception. On the other hand, the Calvinian formula lets human and divine causality fully merge with each other, in that it subordinates the former to the latter in such a way that no conflict can arise between them and is in complete accord with the fundamental doctrine of human incapacity. Accordingly, it seems to me that precisely for this reason it does not bear the germ of conflict in itself but simply needs to be expounded unalloyed and guarded from misinterpretations. I believe that I have gathered in outline the otherwise scattered fundamentals necessary to attain that end so that each reader may indeed find one's own reassurance. Otherwise, one would have to demand for oneself that inadmissible freedom that contests not only the doctrine of election but also every idea regarding a higher ordering of the world, and which delivers us up to sheer arbitrariness.[201] Thus, to express the matter in a final word: if God has not foreseen all things, God cannot have foreseen anything.

NOTES

INTRODUCTION

1. The following English translation is from Friedrich Schleiermacher, "Über die Lehre von der Erwählung, besonders in Beziehung auf Herrn Dr. Bretschneiders Aphorismen," *Theologische Zeitschrift* Erstes Heft (Berlin, 1819). Later published in the *Saemtliche Werke, Erste Abteilung, Zur Theologie, Zweiter Band* (Berlin: G. Reimer, 1836), 393–484. And most recently in *Kritische Gesamtausgabe, I.10, Theologisch-dogmatisch Abhandlungen und Gelegenheitsschriften*, ed. Hans-Friedrich Traulsen and Martin Ohst (Berlin, New York: Walter de Gruyter, 1990), 146-222.

2. Augustine, *On Rebuke and Grace*, in *The Works of Saint Augustine, Answer to the Pelagians, IV: To the Monks of Hadrumetum and Provence I/26*, ed. and trans. Roland J. Teske, SJ (New York: New City Press, 1990). For further information about the situation that prompted the writing of *On Rebuke and Grace* see the general introduction to this volume and the essay by James Wetzel, "Predestination, Pelagianism and Foreknowledge," in *The Cambridge Companion to St. Augustine*, ed. Eleonore Stump and Norman Kretzmann (Cambridge: Cambridge University Press, 2001), 50–54.

3. *On Rebuke and Grace*, 113.

4. Ibid., 121.

5. Ibid., 119.

6. Ibid., 120.

7. Ibid.

8. Ibid., 127.

9. Ibid., 126.

10. Ibid., 131.

11. And so James Wetzel notes that the "case of Jesus proves to be the most illuminating for pondering predestination because his is presumably the one case where there is a perfect convergence between what God foreknows and what God predestines." "Predestination, Pelagianism and Foreknowledge," 50.

12. Augustine, *Answer to the Pelagians, IV*, 134.

13. Martin Luther, *Luther's Works*, Volume 33 from Luther's Works, American ed. 55 volumes, ed. Jaroslav Pelikan (vols. 1–30) and Helmut Lehmann (vols. 31–55) (Philadelphia: Fortress; St. Louis: Concordia, 1955–86). Hereafter indicated by LW-.

14. Robert Kolb, *Bound Choice, Election, and the Wittenberg Theological Method: From Martin Luther to the Formula of Concord*, Lutheran Quarterly Books (Grand Rapids: Wm. B. Eerdmans Publishing Co., 2005), 5.

15. LW-25, 371.

16. LW-33, 37, 38.

17. LW-2, 72, 73. Moreover, Kolb notes that "In his dispute with Erasmus in 1525, Luther emphasized God's responsibility more than human responsibility, but that is not the case in many of his sermons, both before 1525 and after, to people he regarded as carelessly disobedient in their daily lives." Kolb, *Bound Choice*, 279.

18. LW-25, 373.

19. Kolb, *Bound Choice*, 274.

20. Philipp Melanchthon (1497–1560) was born Philipp Schwarzert in Baden. Melanchthon studied at Heidelberg and Tübingen. He was trained as a lawyer and was teaching Greek at Wittenberg when he came under the influence of Luther and subsequently studied theology. Melanchthon was a principal leader in the fledgling Reformation movement and was especially instrumental in providing doctrinal clarity to the evangelicals as they worked through Luther's insights. He penned both the Augsburg Confession (1530) and the Apology to the Augsburg Confession (1531). In distinction to Luther's sometimes acerbic style, Melanchthon tended to be even-headed and conciliatory, earning him the nickname *Leisentreter* (he who walks carefully) by Luther, who considered himself indebted to Melanchthon. Melanchthon was hopeful for a rapprochement with the Roman Catholics.

21. Kolb, *Bound Choice*, 278–81.

22. Matthias Flacius (1520–1575) was an important Gnesio-Lutheran voice in the early Lutheran church. After studying at Basel and Tübingen he taught Hebrew at Wittenberg, where he met Melanchthon and came in contact with Reformation theology. After the death of Luther, Flacius considered his to be a faithful interpretation of Luther in his various conflicts with Melanchthon and his followers. Chief and most controversial among these views was his understanding of original sin as constitutive of the essence of the human. Flacius was dismissed from his position at the University of Jena, where he taught New Testament after a twelve-year stay in Magdeburg, where he moved after his conflict with Melanchthon in 1549.

23. Kolb, *Bound Choice*, 77.

24. Prosper taught that God foreknew that the damned would not believe of their own accord. Sin and unbelief, then, were not seen to be the result of the divine decree to the end that this view of foreknowledge "effectively removed the objections to the doctrine of predestination, although embedding the definition of the elect in a doctrine of prescience removed the doctrine itself from any central position." Jaroslav Pelikan, *The Christian Tradition, Volume One, The Emergence of the Catholic Tradition (100–600)* (Chicago: The University of Chicago Press, 1971), 326, 327.

25. Kolb, *Bound Choice*, 193.

26. Ibid., 33.

27. Ibid., 196.

28. Martin Chemnitz (1522–1586) was born in Brandenburg and educated in Frankfurt and Wittenberg, where he lectured on Melanchthon's *Loci Communes*. Chemnitz's importance in the incipient Lutheran church is evident in the role he played in uniting conflicting parties under the Formula of Concord, a Lutheran document that frames the resolution of disputed points in evangelical theology. The Formula of Concord is composed of two parts, the "Epitome" and the "Solid Declaration." The former is a summary of the main points of the latter. This 1577 document was collected with the three ecumenical creeds and earlier Reforma-

tion documents to create the *Book of Concord*, published in 1580. Chemnitz also served as a preacher and church superintendent in the fledgling church. Among his extensive works are found *The Lord's Supper, On the Two Natures, Loci Theologici,* and *Examen Concilii Tridentini* (an examination of the Council of Trent).

29. J. A. O. Preus, "Translator's Preface," in Martin Chemnitz, *The Two Natures in Christ* (St. Louis: Concordia, 1971), 9.

30. Solid Declaration XI.43. Cf. also Luther's claim that fear of not being elect is a sign of election. Cf. LW-25, 377. In addition to addressing the topic of election, the Solid Declaration also addresses original sin, free will, the righteousness of faith, good works, law and gospel, the third use of the law, the Lord's Supper, the person of Christ, Christ's descent into hell, the Lutheran theme of *Adiaphora* (practices in the church without bearing upon doctrine), and other Reformation movements.

31. Brian A. Gerrish, *The Old Protestantism and the New: Essays on the Reformation Heritage* (Edinburgh: T. & T. Clark, 2004), 150.

32. For this reason Barth's insistence on determining the nature of sin christologically is already patent in Calvin. Cf. Gerrish, *The Old Protestantism,* 151.

33. John Calvin, *Institutes of the Christian Religion,* ed. John T. McNeill, trans. Ford Lewis Battles, Library of Christian Classics (Philadelphia: Westminster Press, 1960), 3.22.3.

34. Ibid., 3.23.7.

35. Ibid., 3.23.9.

36. Ibid., 3.23.8; 3.23.2.

37. Ibid., 3.21.6.

38. Ibid., 3.22.1.

39. Gerrish, *The Old Protestantism and the New,* 144.

40. *Inst.,* 3.22.1.

41. "Indeed, 'secret' (*arcanum*) remains Calvin's most characteristic description for God's 'design' (his *consilium*), since we cannot always perceive *why* God moves events in just the way he does." Gerrish, *The Old Protestantism and the New,* 141.

42. *Inst.,* 3.22.1.

43. Ibid., 3.23.12.

44. Ibid., 3.14.6; 3.14.2.

45. Ibid., 3.21.7.

46. Ibid., 3.23.1. Here Calvin writes: ". . . those whom God passes over, he condemns; and this he does for no other reason than that he wills to exclude them from the inheritance which he predestines for his own children."

47. Cf. Karl Gottlieb Bretschneider, *Aphorismen über die Union der beiden evangelischen Kirchen in Deutschland, ihre gemeinschaftliche Abendmahlsfeier und den Unterschied ihrer Lehre (Auszug),* in *Friedrich Schleiermacher Kritische Gesamtausgabe, I.10 (KGA I.10),* ed. Hans-Friedrich Traulsen and Martin Ohst (Berlin: Walter de Gruyter, 1990), 444–68.

48. "Bretschneider" in *Realencyklopädie für protestantische Theologie und Kirche: Dritter Band,* ed. D. Albert Hauck (Leipzig: J. C. Hinrichsische Buchhandlung, 1897), 389–91.

49. Ibid.

50. Ibid., 391.

51. Bretschneider, *Aphorismen,* 446, 447.

52. Ibid., 445, 446.

53. Ibid., 448.

54. Ibid., 449.

55. Ibid., 452. Bretschneider claims that all scriptural allusions to God's hardening of hearts reference natural rather than spiritual consequences.

56. Ibid., 455.

57. Rom. 7:21.

58. Bretschneider, *Aphorismen*, 457–59.

59. Ibid., 461.

60. Ibid., 448, 463.

61. This argument is buttressed by the observation that just as a person does not cease to be a person after birth, neither does a religious person after rebirth cease in the new life (see p. 64 below).

62. *On the Doctrine of Election*, p. 131n38. "Previously provided for" translates Schleiermacher's *vorhergesehen*, which in tandem with *vorher versehen* underscore God as the one who both establishes the conditions for all that happens in the world and the realization of what does occur, including resistance to God.

63. The *Book of Concord* understands God's mode of knowing in both foreknowledge and election to be active rather than passive. In foreknowledge God limits evil and in election—comprising both foresight and foreknowledge—God knows, in a fashion, what effects salvation. Cf. *Solid Declaration* XI.6, 8. As for Luther, Kolb notes that "God did not foresee what would happen independent of his creative activity, objectively discerning from a distance what happens apart from his involvement, but rather God's creative foreknowing actively determined what the future would be." Kolb, *Bound Choice*, 264. As is evident throughout this work, it is not always clear to what degree Bretschneider considered his to be a Lutheran position or a revisionist Lutheran position.

64. One looks in vain in this monograph for reference to Schleiermacher's signature expression "feeling of absolute dependence," which is related to election in *The Christian Faith*, English Translation of the Second German Edition, ed. H. R. Mackintosh and J. S. Stewart (Edinburgh: T. & T. Clark, 1994), 546. In effect, *On the Doctrine of Election* explicates "feeling of absolute dependence" in the parlance of the tradition.

65. In *The Christian Faith* Schleiermacher asserts God as the author of sin, but not in the same sense as God is the author of redemption. One might propose the former as an indirect authorship. In his description of sin, Schleiermacher proposes that sin occurs in the chasm that separates God's commanding and efficient will. This separation, however, is the sphere of human action. God is not the author of sin by virtue of act but by virtue of God's willing that God's efficient will should not attain to his commanding will. Cf. *The Christian Faith*, §81:332.

66. *Vorherversehung*. Cf. note 62 above.

67. Cf. *The Christian Faith*, §120:558, where Schleiermacher asserts that election is not about individuals, but about humanity as a whole.

68. In a like manner, Schleiermacher's latter phenomenology of religious life parallels this explication insofar as our experience of freedom and dependence as mutually related trade on our status as absolutely dependent. Cf. *The Christian Faith*, §4:12–18.

69. Schleiermacher uses the metaphor of concentric circles in which he asserts that "all other fellowships of faith are destined to pass into the Christian fellowship." *The Christian Faith*, §117:536.

70. Schleiermacher notes that humankind's progress in redemption is akin to the individual's experience of sanctification. The *telos* of that activity is reached when the totality of new creation is equal to the general mass. *The Christian Faith,* §118.1:540, §119.3:550, 551.

71. And so the distinction between the reprobate and the redeemed is one constituted by temporality, which allows Schleiermacher to assert that "they are just where the whole Church was to begin with. On this account we can never cease to regard them as objects of the same divine activity that gathered the Church together, and as embraced along with us all under the same divine fore-ordination." *The Christian Faith,* §119.2:548.

72. This Greek word, found in Eph. 1:10, points to the act of God in Christ whereby all things are gathered together under the headship of Christ.

73. Matthias Gockel, "New Perspectives on an Old Debate: Friedrich Schleiermacher's Essay on Election," *International Journal of Systematic Theology* 6, no. 3 (July 2004): 301.

74. Bruce McCormack considers Barth's treatment of election to be his greatest contribution to the development of church doctrine. Cf. "Grace and Being: The Role of God's Gracious Election in Karl Barth's Theological Ontology," in *The Cambridge Companion to Karl Barth,* ed. John Webster (Cambridge: Cambridge University Press, 2000), 92.

75. Karl Barth, *Church Dogmatics* II/2, *The Doctrine of God,* ed. G. W. Bromiley and T. F. Torrance, trans. G. W. Bromiley et al. (Edinburgh: T. & T. Clark, 1957). Hereafter indicated by *CD.*

76. After all, theology is the memory of the church according to Bonhoeffer. Cf. Dietrich Bonhoeffer, *Dietrich Bonhoeffer Works, Volume 2, Act and Being,* ed. Wayne Whitson Floyd Jr., trans. H. Martin Rumscheidt (Minneapolis: Fortress Press, 1996), 130.

77. *CD* II/2, 3, 103.

78. *CD* II/2, 183, 184.

79. McCormack, "Grace and Being," 97.

80. *CD* II/2, 162.

81. *CD* II/2, 25, 43.

ON THE DOCTRINE OF ELECTION

1. From Doctor Wiggers in Rostock and from Prof. Twesten in Kiel. [Ed. note: August Detlev Christian Twesten (1789–1876) was a professor of theology who was active in his academic career up to the date of his death. He studied philosophy and philology at *Die Kieler Universität* and theology at *Die Berliner Universität,* where he was among the first of Schleiermacher's students. He taught systematic theology and philosophy at Kiel. After declining a call to Bonn, he advanced as rector at Kiel, where he moved catechesis out of the department of pastoral theology and established "pedagogy" as a freestanding discipline. He is known for his efforts in applying the insights of Schleiermacher to the foundation and life of the church at his time. Cf. *Realencyklopädie für Theologie und Kirche, Zwanziger Band,* ed. Albert Hauck (Leipzig: J. C. Hinrichs'sche Buchhandlung, 1908), 171–76. Gustav Friedrich Wiggers (1777–1860) was born near Rostock. He was educated at

Göttingen, where he served as a *Privatdozent* before becoming professor of theology and church history. Two of his works appeared in English: *A Life of Socrates* (London: Taylor and Walton, 1811) and *An Historical Presentation of Augustinianism and Pelagianism from the Original Sources*, trans. Rev. Ralph Emerson (Andover: Gould, Newman and Saxton, 1840).]

2. Ed. note: *Entshuldigung.*

3. Ed. note: Gottschalk (der Sachse) 806/8–866/70 was a strict double predestinarian who was strongly influenced by Augustine's doctrine but who differed from him in developing his position on the basis of divine immutability. See *Theologische Realenzyklopedie*, vol. 14, Knut Schaeferdiek (Berlin: Walter de Gruyter, 1985), 108–10.

4. Ed. note: *Lehrsatz.* Note that Schleiermacher divides the *Glaubenslehre* as follows: *Teil, Abschnitt, Hauptstück, Lehrstück,* and *Lehrsatz.*

5. Ed. note: Rom. 7:24.

6. Ed. note: Acts 10:35.

7. Ed. note: e.g. 1 Cor. 15:10.

8. Ed. note: John. 3:1–10.

9. Ed. note: Rom. 7:25.

10. Ed. note: *dieses mehrere.*

11. Ed. note: *eigentümlichen inneren Erfahrungen.*

12. Although one cannot quote here at length, still the whole of Luther must be summarized. For this purpose in place of all others the following words from the Preface to the Commentary on the Epistle to the Galatians serves the purpose: "For in my heart there rules this one doctrine, namely, faith in Christ. From it, through it, and to it all my theological thought flows and returns day and night." And he further describes this theme as the "single solid rock which we call the doctrine of justification, namely, that we are redeemed from sin, death, and the devil and endowed with eternal life, not through ourselves and certainly not through our works, which are even less than we are ourselves, but through the help of Another, the only Son of God, Jesus Christ." WA VIII, pp. 1524, 1525. [Ed. note: Schleiermacher cites *D. Martin Luthers Sämtliche Schriften, Band 8* (Halle: J. G. Walch, 1742). Here we have cited the American Edition (Luther's Works Volume 27, ed. Jaroslav Pelikan and Walter A. Hansen (St. Louis: Concordia, 1964), 145. This latter translates *D. Martin Luthers Werke Kritische Gesamtausgabe 40. Band Erste Abteilung* (Weimar: Hermann Böhlaus Nachfolger, 1911), 33.]

13. Ed. note: *Gnadenwahl.*

14. Ed. note: Here Schleiermacher uses the word *discors* suggesting an absence of harmony. The *Book of Concord* (1580) contains the three ecumenical creeds and seven confessional documents of the Lutheran church, including the Formula of Concord (1577), which contains two parts, the Epitome and the Solid Declaration. The former is a summary of the latter. The Formula of Concord addresses contentious issues in the life of the nascent Lutheran church through the lens of The Augsburg Confession (1530) and the Apology of the Augsburg Confession (1531), both of which are also in the *Book of Concord.*

15. Gerh., loc. th. T. IV, §162. ". . . who from eternity, in his infallible knowledge, ordained that the believer, resting in Christ by grace of the Holy Spirit through the hearing of the gospel is elect or predestined to life." [Ed. note: on Gerhard see editor's note 20 below. Schleiermacher references the Cotta edition. Cf. also Johann Gerhard, *Locorum Theologicorum Tomus Secundus* (Lipsiae: J. C. Hin-

richs, 1885), 56.] In the Confessions themselves, however, this is not found with the same certainty, but most nearly approaches this in Solid Declaration.XI.40: "Therefore God . . . has ordained that the Holy Spirit calls the elect by the Word . . . and all those who embrace Christ in true faith he justifies . . . thus in the same place, he has decreed by his counsel that he will harden, scorn and condemn to eternal damnation those who reject him who calls by that word . . . and resist the Holy Spirit." [Ed. note: Schleiermacher cites the text as reading *repudiare* (scorn) when in fact it reads *reprobare*. See footnote 16 regarding the Solid Declaration.] This cannot really easily agree with the strong Augustinian formula, particularly as formulated in Solid Declaration.XI.30: "*. . . who are ordained according to the purpose obtaining an inheritance*: they hear the gospel, believe in Christ . . . etc." [Ed. note: The italicized portion represents the Confessors' paraphrase of Eph. 1:11. Also note that Schleiermacher has read *ad capessendam haereditatem* for *ad capiendam hereditatem*.] But the above doctrine can easily be developed out of this, which is the intent of the orthodox doctrine of the Lutheran Church.

16. Ed. note: "*Per verbum . . . donatur spiritus sanctus, qui fidem efficit ubi et quando visum est Deo in iis qui audiunt evangelium.*" Augsburg Confession, v. 2. For the Latin and German text cf. *Concordia Triglotta: The Symbolic Books of the Evangelical Lutheran Church. German-Latin-English* (St. Louis: Concordia Publishing House, 1921). Hereafter the Augsburg Confession, the Apology of the Augsburg Confession, the Epitome, and the Solid Declaration from the *Book of Concord* will be abbreviated as AC, AP, EP, and SD with the article following in roman numerals and the paragraph in arabic. In what follows, the editors have provided translations since Schleiermacher sometimes deviates from or abbreviates the Latin text. Readers are referred to *The Book of Concord: The Confessions of the Evangelical Lutheran Church*, ed. Robert Kolb and Timothy J. Wengert (Minneapolis: Fortress Press, 2000) for contemporary translations and introductions.

17. Ed. note: *contemtus Dei*. Cf. AP.II.8. The Latin text actually uses *contemptum Dei*.

18. Ed. note: *Aufhebung*.

19. Ed. note: SD.XI. 57, 60. See introduction, note 30.

20. Ed. note: in abbreviation, Schleiermacher cites the quotations adduced here, first citing the Cotta edition of Johann Gerhard's *Loci Theologici* (Tübingen, 1768), § 162. Cf. also Johann Gerhard, *Locorum Theologicorum Tomus Tertius* (Lipsiae: J. C. Hinrichs, 1885), 410. Johann Gerhard (1582–1637) was deemed to be the preeminent theologian of the period of Lutheran orthodoxy. Gerhard served as superintendent in Heldburg and general superintendent in Coburg before becoming professor at Jena in 1616. He studied at Wittenberg, Jena, and Marburg. His most famous work is the *Loci Theologici* in nine volumes, cited here by Schleiermacher.

21. Ed. note: Franz Volkmar Reinhard, *Vorlesungen über die Dogmatik* (Amberg-Sulzbach: Seidel, 1801), 464. In contradistinction to the rationalists, Reinhard (1753–1812) saw reason at its best in relationship to revelation, wherein the latter limited the former. He was famed as court preacher at Dresden and served as professor at Wittenberg.

22. Ed. note: Philipp Konrad Marheineke, *Die Grundlehren der christlichen Dogmatik* (Berlin: F. Dümmler, 1819), 416. Marheineke (1780–1846) was professor at Göttingen, Heidelberg, and Berlin in dogmatics and symbolics. Marheineke was Schleiermacher's Lutheran colleague in ministry at the Church of the Triune God

in Berlin. He was increasingly sympathetic to Hegel, as became evident in later editions of *Die Grundlehren.*

23. Ed. note: Wilhelm Martin Leberecht de Wette, *Lehrbuch der christlichen Dogmatik, in ihrer historischen Entwickelung dargestellt, Zweyter Theil. Die Dogmatik der lutherischen Kirche enthaltend* (Berlin: G. Reimer, 1831), 172. W. M. L. de Wette (1780–1849) was professor of Old Testament at Basel. He was especially influenced by Gottlob Paulus, an extreme rationalist.

24. Ed. note: *Einwirkung.*

25. Ed. note: *Einwirkungen.*

26. SD.XI.41. "This contempt of the Word is not caused by the foreknowledge or predestination of God, but in the perverse will [ed. note: *voluntas*] of the human . . . which . . . opposes . . . the Holy Spirit." Cf. also Gerh., *locc. th. T. IV,* § 167. [Ed. note: Schleiermacher cites the Cotta Edition. Cf. also Gerhard, *Locorum Theologicorum Tomus Secundus* (Lipsiae: J. C. Hinrichs, 1885), 59–60.]

27. Storr, *doctr. christ.* § 116. ". . . nor do pious sensibilities, whose rise and liveliness are supported and defended by divine aid against the conflicting tyranny of desire shrink from the proof of the precepts of doctrine, nor from the nature of human morality, but are consonant with the understanding of doctrine . . . insofar as possible for humans . . . so that it is either possible to behold them, to grow in them, and to follow them and so to act in agreement with established doctrine and adjunct sensibilities, or it is possible to neglect and suppress good sensibilities." [Ed. note: Gottlob Christianus Storr, *Doctrinae christianae pars theoretica e sacris literis repetita* (Stuttgardiae: J. B. Metzler, 1807), 323. Storr (1746–1805) held a master's degree in philosophy from Tübingen before taking his theological exams. He taught in the faculty of philosophy in Tübingen before receiving his doctorate in theology, at which point he taught there in the faculty of theology. Storr also served as a *Stadtpfarrer* and *Spezialsuperintendent* in the Stuttgart ministerium. His *Doctrinae christianae* remained authoritative as a system for those seeking a conservative theology with apologetic and evangelical themes. Storr took leave of the older Tübingen school with its orthodox substructure by means of a "biblical supranaturalism" with its direct appeal to biblical authority as a foundation for a scientific theology deriving a system from scripture by means of logic. Cf. *The Schaff-Herzog Encyclopedia of Religious Knowledge,* vol. 12, ed. Samuel Macauley Jackson (Grand Rapids: Baker, 1950), 34, 35.]

28. Ed. note: *Empfindungen.*

29. Ed. note: The reference is to Storr; cf. footnote 27.

30. Ed. note: *Persönlichkeit.*

31. Proceeding on the basis of our premise, which theologians would not subscribe with complete conviction to what Calvin has to say about this in *Inst.* 3.2.4 and also in 2.3.1 in the words, "Accordingly, whatever is not spiritual in man is by this reckoning called 'carnal.' We have nothing of the Spirit, however, except through regeneration. Whatever we have from nature, therefore, is flesh." [Ed. note: John Calvin, *Institutes of the Christian Religion,* ed. John T. McNeill, trans. Ford Lewis Battles, Library of Christian Classics (Philadelphia: Westminster Press, 1960), 289.]

32. Ed. note: *ob er sie vernachlässigen wird.*

33. Ed. note: *Empfindungen.*

34. "Just as, then, they are forced to admit that it is a gift of God that someone finishes this life before changing from good to evil, though they do not know

why God gives this to some and not to others, so . . . perseverance in the good is a gift of God . . . etc." St. Augustine, *On Rebuke and Grace* [Ed. note: in *The Works of St. Augustine I/26: Answer to the Pelagians, IV: To the Monks of Hadrumetum and Provence*, ed. John E. Rostelle, OSA, trans. Roland J. Teske, SJ (New York: New City Press, 1999), § 19.] Therefore, evidently the same must apply with regard to the transition from evil to good.

35. Ed. note: *Inst.* 3.23.7.

36. Ammon, *Glükkwünschungsschreiben.* [Ed. note: Christoph Friedrich Ammon, *Über die Hoffnung einer freien Vereinigung beider protestantischen Kirchen. Ein Glükkwünschungsschreiben an den Herren Antistes Dr. Heß in Zürich bei der bevorstehenden dritten Jubelfeier der schweitzerischen Reformation* (Hannover/Leipzig: Hahn, 1818), 62. Having held professorships in Erlangen and Göttingen Christoph Friedrich von Ammon (1766–1850) was thereafter appointed Court Chaplain (*Oberhofprediger*) in Dresden in 1813. Schleiermacher was sharply critical of Ammon's evasive posturings with regard to the matter of church union. See Schleiermacher's *An Herrn Oberhofprediger D. Ammon über seine Prüfung der Harmischen Sätze* (1818) in KGA I.10, 17–92, Zugabe, 96–116. ET: Iain G. Nicol, *Schleiermacher on Creeds, Confessions and Church Union* (Lewiston, New York: The Edwin Mellen Press, 2004), 65–160.]

37. Augustine, *On Rebuke and Grace*, 139, 140. Cf. *Enchiridion*, "Furthermore, who would be so impiously foolish as to say that God cannot turn the evil wills of men—as he willeth, when he willeth, and where he willeth—toward the good?" Augustine, *Enchiridion* [Ed. note: in Library of Christian Classics, vol. 12, *Augustine: Confessions and Enchiridion*, trans. and ed. Albert C. Outler (Philadelphia: Westminster Press, 1955), 396].

38. Calvin *Inst.* 1.16.2: "But anyone who has been taught by Christ's lips . . . will consider that all events are governed by God's secret plan." Also 1.16.4: "Whence, it follows that providence is lodged in the act; for many babble too ignorantly of bare foreknowledge." [Ed. note: "already preordained" translates *vorher versehen ware.*]

39. Ed. note: *Gnadenwahl.*

40. Ed. note: *Probe.*

41. "For what do we accomplish when, relying upon every vain assurance, we consider, plan, try, and undertake what we think is fitting; then—while in our very first efforts we are actually forsaken by and destitute of sane understanding as well as true virtue—we nonetheless rashly press on until we hurtle to destruction? Yet for those confident they can do anything by their own power, things cannot happen otherwise." (*Inst.* 2.1.2).

42. Ed. note: See, e.g., Rom. 6:1–2.

43. Ed. note: See, e.g., Rom. 8:16, 21.

44. Ed. note: *im gläubigen Vertrauen.*

45. Augustine, *On Rebuke and Grace*, § 12. ". . . and those who, though they were changed for the better after hearing it (the gospel) did not receive perseverance . . . have not been set apart from the mass which, it is certain has been condemned . . ." (§ 16). "But those who are not going to persevere and thus are going to fall away from the Christian faith and way of life so that the end of this life finds them in that state are undoubtedly not to be counted in the number of these chosen ones, even at the time when they were living good and pious lives" (§ 20). "And there are also some people who are called children of God by us on account of the

grace they received, at least for a time, but they are, nonetheless, not such in the eyes of God (1 John 2:19)" (§ 22). "Because, therefore, they did not have persever-ance . . . so they were not truly children of God . . ."

46. Augustine, *On Rebuke and Grace* § 25: "But since the one who gives the rebuke does not know whether he was called in that way, let him do with love what he knows he must do, for he knows that he must rebuke such a person and that God will bring about either mercy or judgment." § 46: "For, not knowing who pertains and does not pertain to the number of the predestined, we ought to have such a spirit of love that we want all to be saved."

47. Ed. note: See John 10:12–13.

48. ". . . when man has been taught that no good thing remains in his power . . . in spite of this he should nevertheless be instructed to aspire to a good of which he is empty, to a freedom of which he has been deprived." (*Inst.* 2.2.1).

49. "If election has as its goal holiness of life, it ought rather to arouse and goad us eagerly to set our mind upon it than to serve as a pretext for doing noth-ing." (*Inst.* 3.23.12).

50. Ed. note: John 3:15.

51. Ed. note: *Aphorisms*, 103.

52. Ed. note: SD.XI.1–3, 17–22.

53. "But they stretch their blasphemies farther when they say that he who has been condemned by God, if he endeavors through innocent and upright life to make himself approved of God (cf. 2 Tim. 2:15), will lose his labor. In this con-tention they are convicted of utterly shameless falsehood. Whence could such endeavor arise but from election?" (*Inst.* 3.23.12).

54. Ed. note: Rom. 10:9.

55. Ed. note: Rom. 7:22.

56. "If we confess that we lack what we seek of God, . . . no one should now hesitate to confess that he is able to understand God's mysteries only in so far as he is illumined by God's grace." (*Inst.* 2.2.21).

57. Precisely this is expressly maintained by many Lutheran theologians and indeed most recently by Mr. Ammon, *Glükkwünschungsschreiben*, 40. Cf. also the words of EP.IV.19: "Further, we reject and condemn the doctrine that faith in Christ is not lost and that the Holy Spirit dwells in the human no less even if one knowingly and willingly sins." SD.XI.20: "So, too, in God's eternal counsel, God purposed to protect the one justified yet still feeble in many and various ways against the devil, the world, and the flesh . . . and if such a one falls, God will pro-vide a hand of support."

58. Cf. Dr. Ammon *op. cit.*, 61.

59. "But if we have been chosen in him [Christ], we shall not find assurance of our election in ourselves; and not even in God the Father, if we conceive him as severed from his Son. Christ, then, is the mirror wherein we must, and without self-deception may, contemplate our own election." (*Inst.* 3.24.5).

60. "Even though discussion about predestination is likened to a dangerous sea, still, in traversing it, one finds safe and calm—I also add pleasant—sailing unless he willfully desire to endanger himself." (*Inst.* 3.24.4).

61. "Therefore, . . . we shall be following the best order if, in seeking the cer-tainty of our election, we cling to those latter signs which are sure attestations of it." (*Inst.* 3.24.4).

62. Ed. note: *ob er mit Christo in Gemeinschaft stehe.*

63. ". . . we have sufficiently clear and firm testimony that we have been inscribed in the book of life (cf. Rev. 21:27) if we are in communion with Christ." (*Inst.* 3.24.5).

64. *Inst.* 1.6.1.

65. "Now among the elect we regard the call as a testimony of election. Then we hold justification another sign of its manifestation, until they come into the glory in which the fulfillment of that election lies." (*Inst.* 3.21.7).

66. "Now there is no doubt, when Christ prays for all the elect, that he implores for them the same thing as he did for Peter, that their faith may never fall (Luke 22:32). From this we infer that they are out of danger of falling away because the Son of God, asking that their godliness be kept constant, did not suffer a refusal. What did Christ wish to have us learn from this but to trust that we shall ever remain safe because we have been made his once for all?" (*Inst.* 3.24.6).

67. Ed. note: *Buchstaben*.

68. Ed. note: John 3:8.

69. In no respect do I want to ascribe to this designation the force of an accusation of heresy. I also understand it as referring not only to the strict form of Pelagianism but rather to all its different forms in which it has departed from the teaching of Augustine.

70. Ed. note: i.e., the Lutherans.

71. EP.XI.9: "Therefore the true meaning of predestination must be learned from the Gospel of Christ. A godly person can only advance this far safely, by reflecting on this article concerning the eternal election of God insofar as it is manifestly revealed in the Word of God . . . other thoughts are to be driven out entirely." SD.XI.43: "Sacred Scripture advances to this point in revealing the mystery of divine predestination. If we continue within these boundaries . . . this doctrine truly offers us a subject matter most full of consolation. . . . Indeed, all false suppositions and erroneous doctrines concerning the natural power of our will [Ed. note: *arbitrii*] are overthrown since it is clear that God, in his counsel before the ages of this world, determined and ordained that the self-same God wills to work and effect in us by the power of God's Holy Spirit through the Word all that pertains to our conversion."

72. Ed. note: *Einsicht*.

73. Ed. note: *durch den geselligen*.

74. Ed. note: *Gottes Regierung*.

75. Ed. note: *sie löse die moralische Natur auf*.

76. Ed. note: *um die Willkühr Gottes zu erheben*.

77. Ed. note: *die heiligen Männer Gottes*.

78. Ed. note: *vorgegebenen*, i.e. supposed or would-be.

79. Ed. note: *wie Gott berechnet hat*.

80. Ed. note: *Vorherversehung*, i.e. providing for, in advance.

81. SD.XI.4, 5. "Indeed, foreknowledge or foreseeing . . . extends over creatures, both good and bad. . . . Truly, eternal election, or the predestination of God to salvation does not pertain at once to good and evil persons but only to the children of God, who were consequently elect and ordained to eternal life before the foundation of the world was laid."

82. Rom. 11:11–24.

83. Ed. note: i.e., acceptance.

84. Ed. note: i.e., rejection.

85. Ed. note: *Gegenstand.*

86. Ed. note: i.e., transgression.

87. Ed. note: i.e., salvation.

88. Rom. 5:12–19.

89. Ed. note: *durch.*

90. Ed. note: *rein und gleich.*

91. Ed. note: i.e., all humans (plural genitive).

92. Ed. note: i.e., kings. The Greek text is actually in the genitive, although it is cited here in the nominative.

93. Ed. note: i.e., those having prominence; more generally understood and translated as rulers. Here the Greek text reads, *tōn en huperoxē ontōn.*

94. Ed. note: i.e., all humans (in the plural accusative case).

95. Ed. note: *Ausdruck.*

96. Ed. note: Matt. 28:18–20.

97. Ed. note: Rom. 1:20.

98. Ed. note: *selig werden.*

99. Ed. note: John 14:3.

100. Ed. note: Matt. 22:14.

101. Ed. note: Augustine, *On Rebuke and Grace,* 140.

102. Ed. note: Rom. 3:23; 5:12. The quotation is found in *Aphorismen,* 98, as found in *Friedrich Daniel Ernst Schleiermacher Kritische Gesamtausgabe, Erste Abteilung, Schriften und Entwürfe, Bande 10,* ed. Hans-Friedrich Traulsen and Martin Ost (Berlin: Walter de Gruyter, 1990), 458.

103. Ed. note: Rom. 5:17: "those receiving the abundance of grace will rule in life."

104. Ed. note: "for all."

105. "For few accept the Word of God earnestly and conform to it in sincerity. Indeed many initially receive the Word of God with great joy, but afterwards fall away again." [Ed. note: Luke 8:13] SD.XI.41, 43.

106. Ed. note: Ammon. Cf. p. 91n36 above.

107. Ed. note: SD.XI.57: "*Gott schenke manchen Völkern und Reichen sein Wort nicht, oder nehme es ihnen wieder.*" Here Schleiermacher paraphrases in reference to both the German and Latin texts from the first sentence of paragraph 57 of The Solid Declaration. Cf. "*Gleichfalls, wenn wir sehen daß Gott sein Wort an einem Ort gibt, an dem andern nicht gibt, von einen Ort hinwegnimmt, an andern bleiben läßt*" and "*Ad eundem modum cum videmus, quod Deus verbum suum alicui regno aut ditioni donat idem vero alii genti non largitur; item quod id ipsum ab uno populo aufert, alii vero diutius concedit.*" *Triglotta,* 1080.

108. ". . . we see that God does not lavish . . . God's Word to other people; likewise, that God removes the same from a people . . ."—". . . God owes absolutely nothing to us . . ."—"Therefore, he displays his righteous judgment which, in certain reigns, nations, people, is merited by the impious person." SD.XI.57, 60.

109. "However, regarding any ideas or speech that soars [so as] to stray beyond these limits in this debate, we should hold these [limits] fast and with St. Paul put our hand over our mouth, mindful to say: 'who are you, human, who answers back to God?'" [Ed. note: Rom. 9:20.] SD.XI.63.

110. *Huper hapantōn gar apethanen eis to sōsai pantas to autou meros. Ou pantōn de tas hamartias anānegke, dia to mā pantas pisteusai.* Chrys. ad Ebr. IX, 28. T XII,

§ 168. [Ed. note: As regards all—for he died for the salvation of all, a part of which, however, are not forgiven their sins since all do not believe.]

111. Ed. note: Augustine, *On Rebuke and Grace*, 143. Cf. 2 Cor. 13:4.

112. What Dr. Bretschneider cites (p. 112) from Article XI of the *Expositio Simplex* can and must be accepted by all orthodox Lutherans if only they seek to discover nothing other behind its expression than what they actually contain, for here both are juxtaposed, namely the sufficiency of the power and the limited nature of the outcome. [Ed. note: Here Schleiermacher is referring to Article XI, 16 of the Second Helvetic Confession of 1566. See, e.g., Philip Schaff, *The Creeds of Christendom*, vol. 3 (New York: Harper and Bros., 1877), 257.]

113. Given that Dr. Bretschneider expressly demonstrates from the Second Helvetic Confession that it does not state that God elected all human beings to blessedness, an uninformed person might easily conclude that this is what the Lutheran Church says. However, it also says, "This eternal plan is that . . . all who are truly repentant and embrace Christ in true faith God wills to justify." SD.XI.18. Further, "Likewise, God ordained in his eternal counsel that those whom he elects . . . he wills to save and to adorn with eternal glory." SD.XI.22.

114. Ed. note: *in der Idee.*

115. Ed. note: *Beseligung.*

116. Cf. Gerhard, op. cit., Tome III, 201. [Ed. note. Schleiermacher cites the Cotta Edition. Cf. also Gerhard, *Locorum Theologicorum Tomus Primus* (Lipsiae: J. C. Hinrichs, 1885), 359: "*Antecedens voluntas est, qua Deus ut benignissimus pater omnes homines vult salvos fieri et ad agnitionem veritatis venire, consequens voluntas est, qua Deus ut justissimus judex finaliter impoenitentes et incredulos vult damnari.*"]

117. Ed. note: *selig werden.*

118. *Inst.* 1.18.4: "(God's) will is wrongly confused with his precept: innumerable examples clearly show how utterly different these two are." If this distinction is clear then it is readily understood that in all cases and without any exception the divine intention and the actual outcome do not differ from each other but are always one and the same.

119. Ed. note: *aufheben.*

120. Instead of all the other passages from Augustine that could be cited, this particular one is quoted here: "Hence the words, 'God wills all human beings to be saved' (1 Tim. 2:4) can also be understood in the sense that he makes us will this. . . ." Augustine, *On Rebuke and Grace*, § 47.

121. Ed. note: *Anschauung.*

122. Ed. note: *begnadigt;* i.e., literally made objects of grace.

123. Ed. note: *begnadigt.*

124. Ed. note: *hervorbringen.*

125. Against this Calvin states, "(God) foresees future events only by reason of the fact that he decreed that they take place . . ." (*Inst.* 3.23.6).

126. Ed. note: *zwischen eigentlicher und nicht eigentlicher.*

127. Ed. note: *eigentlich.*

128. *Inst.* 1.18.1: ". . . from these it is more than evident that they babble and talk absurdly who, in place of God's providence, substitute bare permission— as if God sat in a watchtower awaiting chance events, and his judgments thus depended upon human will."

129. Ed. note: *ein Nichtverhindernwollen.*

130. Ed. note: *Anordnung*.

131. Ed. note: Ps. 95:7b–8a.

132. And this is the statement of the French Confession of Faith, § VIII (1559), cited by Dr. Bretschneider (*Aphorisms*, p. 112), with which he finds fault: ". . . but (God) hath wonderful means of so making use of devils and sinners that he can turn to good the evil which they do, and of which they are guilty." [Ed. note: See Philip Schaff, *The Creeds of Christendom*, vol. 3, p. 364.]

133. And it is precisely for this reason that I cannot see how the *ordinavit* [Ed. note: "he ordained"] with regard to the fall can be denied (see *Aphor.*, 113), for otherwise, redemption, which is God's greatest work, must merely be based on an act of permission.

134. Ed. note: *Milderung*.

135. Ed. note: *Gemüth*.

136. Ed. note: *begnadigt*.

137. Ed. note: *Vorherversehung*.

138. Ed. note: *Bestimmung*.

139. "We call predestination God's eternal decree by which he compacted with himself what he willed to become of each man." (*Inst.* 3.21.5). "As Scripture, then, clearly shows, we say that God once established by his eternal and unchangeable plan those whom he long before determined once for all to receive into salvation, and those whom, on the other hand, he would devote to destruction." (*Inst.* 3.21.7).

140. "And it ought not to seem absurd for me to say that God not only foresaw that fall of the first man, and in him the ruin of his descendants, but also meted it out in accordance with his own decision." (*Inst.* 3.23.7). "Still, it is not in itself likely that man brought destruction upon himself through himself, by God's mere permission and without any ordaining. As if God did not establish the condition in which he wills the chief of his creatures to be!" (*Inst.* 3.23.8).

141. "But it was because his will was capable of being bent to one side or the other, and was not given the constancy to persevere, that he fell so easily." (*Inst.* 1.15.8).

142. ". . . nor was it reasonable for God to be constrained by the necessity of making a man who either could not or would not sin at all. Such a nature would, indeed, have been more excellent. But to quarrel with God on this precise point, as if he ought to have conferred this upon man, is more than iniquitous, inasmuch as it was in his own choice to give whatever he pleased." (*Inst.* 1.15.8).

143. "Hence, we confess . . . that God . . . who knew that it pertains to his omnipotent goodness to make good use of evils rather than not to allow evils to exist ordered the life of . . . human beings in such way that he might, first of all, show in their lives what their free choice could do and then what the benefit of his grace . . . could do." Augustine, *On Rebuke and Grace*, § 28.

144. Ed. note: *Begnadigung*.

145. ". . . let our law of soberness . . . be to assent . . . that his will may be for us . . . the truly just cause of all things. Not, indeed, that absolute will of which the Sophists babble, by an impious and profane distinction separating his justice from his power—but providence, that determinative principle of all things, from which flows nothing but right. . . ." (*Inst.* 1.17.2).

146. Ed. note: The Reformed Confession of Electoral Prince Sigismund of Mark Brandenburg (1614). It was to this confession that Schleiermacher subscribed when he was ordained after passing his theological exams in 1790.

147. Ed. note: *nach einem Gutdünken.*

148. Gerhard, op. cit., T. VIII, § 52. ". . . God is not moved by anything regarding the dignity of humankind, indeed neither by foreseeing good works nor faith, such that he thereby elects those to eternal life." [Ed. note: cf. also Gerhard, *Loci Theologici Tomus Secundus* (Lipsiae: J. C. Hinrichs, 1885), 56.] SD.XI.87, 88: ". . . (it is) manifest that the pure and gracious mercy of Christ . . . saves us, in accord with the plan of God's will. . . . Therefore it is false . . . when it is taught that . . . the cause of divine election is still in us in some way, on account of which God has predestined us to eternal life." That with which Dr. Bretschneider (*Aphor.*, 123) finds fault with regard to the Leipzig Confession is literally no different from what is affirmed here. [Ed. note: Schleiermacher here refers to the colloquy held in Leipzig in 1631 in order to develop a common front in protesting the Edict of Restitution. Reformed and Lutheran participants held discussions using the Augsburg Confession as a common text. A text was produced that noted agreement in certain areas—most notably articles 1–2, 5–9, and 11–28—while noting differences with respect to the communication of attributes, the Eucharist and election. Cf. *The Schaff-Herzog Encyclopedia of Religious Knowledge,* volume 6, ed. Samuel Macauley Jackson (Grand Rapids: Baker, 1953), 445, 446 and *Lutheran Cyclopedia,* ed. Erwin L. Lueker (Saint Louis: Concordia, 1954), 893.]

149. Ed. note: See above, p. 49.

150. AC.II and XVIII.

151. Ed. note: *Mass.*

152. Ed. note: *undenkbar.*

153. Ed. note: *hervorgehn.*

154. Ed. note: AC.XVIII: "Of Free Will."

155. Ed. note: *zusammengesetzte.*

156. Ed. note: *eine solche gemeinsame Person bildet.*

157. *Ontōs ktisis heterā estin· ek tou mā ontos eis to einai parāxthāmen.* (Chrysost. Ed. Montf. T. XI. § 28). [Ed. note: "Indeed there is another creation: we have been given over to that which is from that which is not."]

158. ". . . seeing that he (Christ) alone is the fountain of life, the anchor of salvation . . . (and) since it is into his body the Father has destined those to be engrafted whom he has willed from eternity to be his own, that he may hold as sons all whom he acknowledges to be among his members . . . we are said to put on him (Rom. 13:14), to grow together into him (Eph. 4:15), that we may live because he lives." (*Inst.* 3.24.5). "To sum up: Christ, when he illumines us into faith by the power of his Spirit, at the same time so engrafts us into his body that we become partakers of every good." (*Inst.* 3.2.35).

159. "Let this therefore be the first step, that a man depart from himself . . . (to) what turns the mind of man, empty of its own carnal sense, wholly to the bidding of God's Spirit . . . so that the man himself may no longer live but hear Christ living and reigning within him." (*Inst.* 3.7.1). ". . . because when it has been granted to us to believe in Christ for his sake (Phil. 1:29), then at last we begin to pass over from death into life." (*Inst.* 3.14.6).

160. "For grace alone separates the redeemed from the lost, all having been mingled together in the one mass of perdition, arising from a common cause which leads back to their common origins." (St. Augustine, *Enchiridion*, 398). [Ed. note: Schleiermacher incorrectly ascribes this quotation to paragraph 9, when in fact he quotes from paragraph 99 of the *Enchiridion*.] and ". . . we ought to understand that

no one can be set apart from that mass of perdition which the first Adam caused unless one has (this) gift. . . ." (Augustine, *On Rebuke and Grace*, § 12). "How is it that the church becomes manifest to us from this (doctrine of election) when . . . 'it could not otherwise be found or recognized among creatures since it lies marvelously hidden . . . both within the bosom of a blessed predestination and within the mass of a miserable condemnation?'" [Ed. note: Calvin correctly ascribes this reference to Bernard (*Sermon on the Song of Songs*, lxxviii.4) while Schleiermacher excises this reference in quoting Calvin.] "The elect are gathered into Christ's flock by a call not immediately at birth, and not all at the same time, but according as it pleases God to dispense his grace to them. . . . If you look upon them, you will see Adam's offspring, who savor of the common corruption of the mass." (*Inst.* 3.24.10). Appertaining to this also: "Among the 'multitude' I include even certain distinguished folk, until they become engrafted into the body of the church." (*Inst.* 1.7.5).

161. Ed. note: *Punkte.*

162. Ed. note: *Unpersönlichkeit.*

163. Ed. note: *Bestimmungsgründe.*

164. Ed. note: *aus der Mitte.* I.e., Schleiermacher judged that the Protestant neo-scholastics failed to relate the question of the will of God to the doctrine of human incapacity.

165. Ed. note: *Glaubenslehre*, from *doctrina fidei.*

166. Ed. note: SD.XI.8 underscores faith as the effect of that cause that is God's election.

167. Together with the Reformed church the orthodox Lutheran church of course also affirms this in spite of Luke 13:27 and similar passages (cf. *Aphorisms,* 90). And the question as to whether on this account a person could not attain to blessedness because God had not predestined him to this end is resolved in the following, namely, whether a person can attain to blessedness in spite of the fact that God does not extend to him such operations of grace by means of which a living faith is awakened in him. However, this also is a matter that the orthodox Lutheran church cannot accept.

168. Hence, I also can find no inconsistency (*Aphorisms,* 125) when without departing from the Calvinian doctrine the Thorn Confession affirms that for the elect God has preordained faith as a means. This is on account of the fact that apart from the manner and means of its accomplishment the divine decree is wholly inconceivable. However, the decree of election is only carried into effect by means of faith. [Ed. note: The colloquy at Thorn in Poland (1645) involved Roman Catholics, Calvinists, and Lutherans. The Declaration of Thorn that followed was signed by Roman Catholics and Reformed theologians but not the Lutherans. It sought agreement on the basis of a shared affirmation of the councils of the ancient church but failed to articulate consensus on the question of authority. Cf. "Thorn, Religiongespräche" in *Realencyklopädie für protestantische Theologie und Kirche, 19 Band*, ed. Albert Hauck (Leipzig: J. C. Hinrichs'sche Buchhandlung, 1907), 745–51, and Jaroslav Pelikan, *The Christian Tradition: A History of the Development of Doctrine,* vol. 4, *Reformation of Church and Dogma (1300–1700)* (Chicago: University of Chicago Press, 1984), 337–39.]

169. Ed. note: "the will takes the place of reason."

170. Reinhard, *Dogmatik*, §. 120, 445.

171. "For, whatever (Satan) has that is to be condemned he has derived from his revolt and fall." (*Inst.* 1.14.16). "Yet his choice of good and evil was free . . . until in destroying himself he corrupted his own blessings." (*Inst.* 1.15.8).

172. Ed. note: *Grund*.

173. Ed. note: See, e.g., Rom. 3:20; 5:13.

174. Ed. note: Cf. esp. SD.XI.13.

175. Ed. note: Schleiermacher refers to SD.XI.4, 5 as cited in p. 93n81 above.

176. Ed. note: *geistige Einzelwesen*.

177. Ed. note: *des ihm auf verschiedenen Seiten gegebenen Stoffes*.

178. Ed. note: *Bestimmtheit*.

179. Ed. note: Matt. 9:13; Mark 2:17; Luke 5:32.

180. Ed. note: Rom. 11:25a–26b.

181. [. . .] *ismen tou logou proēgoumenon einai ergon sōzein tous sunetōterous· oikeioteroi gar houtoi para tous ambluterous autōi tugxanousin. All' epei ta apolōlota probata oikou Israēl, para to kat' eklogēn xaritos leimma, ēpeithēsan tōi logōi, dia touto ekseleksato ta mōra tou kosmou k.t.l.* (Ed. Paris. III, § 505.) [Ed. note: ". . . we know the procession of the Word to be a work saving the wise. For these members of the household are found by it to exceed the foolish. But when the perishing sheep of the house of Israel—opposing the remnant chosen by grace [Rom. 11:5]—disobeyed the Word, the foolish of the world were elect on this account."]

182. Together with Augustine I have no hesitation in supporting such a position and find his explanation very compelling. "As long, then, as a thing is being corrupted, there is good in it of which it is being deprived; and in this process, if something of its being remains that cannot be further corrupted, this will then be an incorruptible entity [*natura incorruptibilis*], and to this great good it will have come through the process of corruption. But even if the corruption is not arrested, it still does not cease having some good of which it cannot be further deprived. . . . Wherefore corruption cannot consume the good without also consuming the thing itself." (*Enchiridion*, 4). [Ed. note: Augustine, *Augustine: Confessions and Enchiridion*, 343, 344.] The former certainly calls for some slight improvement, but it is also particularly the latter to which we have to hold and thereby link it with the other well-known opinion, namely, *desiderare gratiam initium est gratiae* [Ed. note: "To desire grace is the beginning of grace."]; and the Calvinian, "For we see implanted in human nature some sort of desire to search out the truth to which man would not at all aspire if he had not already savored it." (*Inst.* 2.2.12).

183. Ed. note: *Gliedern*.

184. Ed. note: *Übersehen*. This word, often translated "overlooked," can also mean "those for whom allowances have been made." This is closer to Schleiermacher's own meaning.

185. Ed. note: *Verworfenen*. Or simply "rejected," i.e., "not chosen." "Reprobate" is used here, because the word is derived from "reprove," an action directed toward someone who has not passed the test, but is directed with a kindly intention to help improve, which seems to match the point being made here. That is, persons not of Christian faith would not have met the temporal criteria, later laid out with greater precision in CF §108, of preparatory grace, of hearing the divine Word of redemption, of repentance, of receptivity to grace, and of the experience of faith, the latter of which for a Christian involves a feeling of absolute dependence on God in community with Christ.

186. Ed. note: *Bestimmtheit*.

187. "... they are seeking to know the causes of God's will, when God's will is itself the cause of everything there is." Aug., *de Genesi c. Man*. [Ed. note: Augustine, *"On Genesis: A Refutation of the Manichees,"* in *The Works of St. Augustine I/13: On Genesis*, trans. Edmund Hill, OP and Matthew O'Connell, ed. John E. Rotelle, OSA (New York: New York City Press, 2002), 42.]

188. Ed. note: Rom. 8:7–8.

189. Ed. note: See *Inst*. 3.23.7, where Calvin admits: "The decree is dreadful indeed, I confess."

190. Ed. note: *Nichtsein*.

191. Ed. note: *auszufüllenden*. Literally "filled out" or "filled up," hence, "completed."

192. Ed. note: *ausfüllt*.

193. Ed. note: *begnadigten*.

194. Ed. note: *Mitgefühl*.

195. Ed. note: *Beistand*.

196. Ed. note: *bildet*.

197. Ed. note: Synod of Dort (Dordrecht), 1618–19, Council of the Reformed Church in the Netherlands.

198. Ed. note: Cf. note 36 on Ammon.

199. Ed. note: Johann Gottlieb Töllner (1724–1774) studied theology at Halle with the intention of doing further academic work. He was delayed in this and served as a tutor and *Feldprediger* at Frankfurt before becoming a lecturer there and then a professor of philosophy and theology in 1760 after attaining his doctorate in theology in 1757. He is a representative of a semi-rationalism shaped simultaneously by Wolff and Halle pietism. Cf. *Realencyklopädie für protestantische Theologie und Kirche, Neunzehnter Band* (Leipzig: J. C. Hinrichs'sche Buchhandlung, 1907), 814–17.

200. Ed. note: *für akroamatisch zu erklären* (*Vermischte Aufsätze*, 2te Sammlung, 1766, 172).

201. Ed. note: *und uns dem blossen Ohngefähr preis giebt*.

SELECT BIBLIOGRAPHY

Augustine. *Augustine: Confessions and Enchiridion*, The Library of Christian Classics, translated and edited by Albert C. Outler. Philadelphia: Westminster Press, 1955.

———. "On Rebuke and Grace." In *The Works of St. Augustine, 1/26: Answer to the Pelagians, IV: To the Monks of Hadrumetum and Provence*. Edited by John E. Rotelle, OSA. Translated and edited by Roland J. Teske, SJ. New York: New City Press, 1999.

———. "On the Predestination of the Saints." In *The Fathers of the Church: A New Translation*, vol. 86. Translated by John A. Mourant and William J. Collinge. Washington: The Catholic University of America Press, 1992.

———. "Two Books on Genesis against the Manichees." In *The Fathers of the Church: A New Translation*, vol. 84. Translated by Roland J. Teske, SJ. Washington: The Catholic University of America Press, 1991.

Barth, Karl. *Church Dogmatics*, II/2. *The Doctrine of God*. Edited by G. W. Bromiley and T. F. Torrance. Translated by G. W.Bromiley et al. Edinburgh: T. and T. Clark, 1957.

Bretschneider, Karl Gottlieb. *Aphorismen über die Union der beiden evangelischen Kirchen in Deutschland, ihre gemeinschaftliche Abendmahlsfeier, und den Unterschied ihrer Lehre*. Gotha, 1819. Extracts from this author's contribution to the matter of election are conveniently made available in the Kritische Gesamtausgabe of Schleiermacher's works (see below KGA I. 10, Appendix, 444–68).

Bowman, Donna. *The Divine Decision: A Process Doctrine of Election*. Louisville, KY: Westminster John Knox Press, 2002.

———. "A Process Reading of Schleiermacher's Doctrine of Election." In *The State of Schleiermacher Scholarship Today: Selected Essays*, edited by Edwina Lawler, Jeffery Kinlaw, and Ruth Drucilla Richardson, 161–79. Lewiston, NY: The Edwin Mellen Press, 2006.

Calvin, John. "Articles concerning Predestination." In *Calvin: Theological Treatises*, The Library of Christian Classics, vol. 22. Edited and translated by J. K. S. Reid. Philadelphia: Westminster Press, 1954, 178–80.

———. "De Aeterna Dei Praedestinatione." In *Corpus Reformatorum: Johannis Calvini Opera quae supersunt Omnia*, vol. 8. New York: Johnson Reprint Co., 1964. ET: *Concerning the Eternal Predestination of God*. Translated by J. K. S. Reid. Cambridge: James Clarke, 1961. Reprint: Louisville, KY: Westminster/John Knox Press, 1997.

———. *Institutes of the Christian Religion,* The Library of Christian Classics, vols. 20 and 21. Edited by John T. McNeill. Translated by Ford Lewis Battles. Philadelphia: Westminster Press, 1960. On election and predestination, see especially book 3, chapters 21—25.

Forde, Gerhard O. *The Captivation of the Will: Luther vs. Erasmus on Freedom and Bondage.* Edited by Steven Paulson. Grand Rapids: Wm. B. Eerdmans Publishing Co., 2005.

Fox, Edward Quinn. "One Eternal and Universal Decree: The Dogmatic Function of Schleiermacher's Doctrine of Election and Its Importance for Reformed Theology." Ph.D. diss., Vanderbilt University, 1999.

Gerrish, Brian A. *The Old Protestantism and the New: Essays on the Reformation Heritage.* Edinburgh: T. & T. Clark Ltd., 2004.

Gockel, Matthias. *Barth and Schleiermacher on the Doctrine of Election: A Systematic-Theological Comparison.* Oxford: Oxford University Press, 2006.

———. "New Perspectives on an Old Debate: Friedrich Schleiermacher's Essay on Election." *International Journal of Systematic Theology* 6, no. 3 (July 2004): 301–18.

Hector, Kevin W. "God's Triunity and Self-Determination: A Conversation with Karl Barth, Bruce McCormack and Paul Molnar." *International Journal of Systematic Theology* 7, no. 3 (July 2005): 246–61.

Kolb, Robert. *Bound Choice, Election, and Wittenberg Theological Method: From Martin Luther to the Formula of Concord.* Grand Rapids: William B. Eerdmans Publishing Co., 2005.

Luther, Martin. "The Disputation Concerning Man (1536)." In *Luther's Works,* Volume 34. Translated by Lewis W. Spitz. Philadelphia: Muhlenberg Press, 1960.

———. "The Freedom of a Christian (1520)." In *Luther's Works,* vol. 31. Translated by Harold J. Grimm. Philadelphia: Fortress Press, 1957.

———. "Heidelberg Disputation (1518)." In *Luther's Works,* vol. 31. Translated by Harold J. Grimm. Philadelphia: Fortress Press, 1957.

———. "On the Bondage of the Will (1526)." In *Luther's Works,* vol. 33. Translated by Philip S. Watson and Benjamin Drewery. Philadelphia: Fortress Press, 1972.

McCormack, Bruce. "Grace and Being: The Role of God's Gracious Election in Karl Barth's Theological Ontology." In *The Cambridge Companion to Karl Barth.* Edited by John Webster. Cambridge: Cambridge University Press, 2000.

Muller, Richard A. *Christ and the Decree: Christology and Predestination in Reformed Theology from Calvin to Perkins.* Grand Rapids: Baker Academic, 2008.

Schleiermacher, Friedrich Daniel Ernst. *The Christian Faith.* Translated by H. R. Mackintosh and J. S. Stewart. Edinburgh: T. and T. Clark, 1928. On the doctrine of election and predestination, see especially paras. 115–20, pp. 532–60.

———. "Über die Lehre von der Erwählung, besonders in Beziehung auf Herrn Dr. Bretschneiders Aphorismen." *Theologische Zeitschrift* Erstes

Heft, Berlin, 1819. Later published in the *Saemtliche Werke, Erste Abteilung, Zur Theologie, Zweiter Band*. Berlin: G. Reimer, 1836, pp. 393–484. And most recently in *Kritische Gesamtausgabe*, I.10, *Theologisch-dogmatisch Abhandlungen und Gelegenheitsschriften*. Edited by Hans-Friedrich Traulsen and Martin Ohst. Berlin, New York: Walter de Gruyter, 1990, 146–222.

Van Driel, Edwin Chr. *Incarnation Anyway: Arguments for Supralapsarian Christology*. Oxford: Oxford University Press, 2008.

Wetzel, James. "Predestination, Pelagianism and Foreknowledge." In *The Cambridge Companion to St. Augustine*. Edited by Eleonore Stump and Norman Kretzmann. Cambridge: Cambridge University Press, 2001.

INDEX